The Servant Songs

A Study in Isaiah

The Servant Songs

by

F. Duane Lindsey

MOODY PRESS
CHICAGO

Dedicated to
my wife Barbara,
constant source of strength as
companion servant of the Sovereign LORD

Except where noted, Scripture is taken from the *Holy Bible: New International Version.* Copyright ©1973, 1978 by the International Bible Society. Used by permission of Zondervan Bible Publishers.

The proper name of God, rendered as "LORD" in most modern versions, is referred to in this commentary as "Yahweh" in text.

Chapters 2 through 5 are a revision of material previously copyrighted by *Bibliotheca Sacra* and are used by permission.

Library of Congress Cataloging in Publication Data

Lindsey, F. Duane, 1934–
    The servant songs.

    Includes indexes.
    1. Bible. O.T. Isaiah XL–LV—Criticism, interpretation, etc. 2. Servant of Jehovah. I. Title.
BS1520.L56 1985   224'.106   85-2929
ISBN 0-8024-4093-2 (pbk.)

    1 2 3 4 5 6 7 Printing/BC/Year 90 89 88 87 86 85

Printed in the United States of America

Contents

Foreword

Probably the clearest and most complete picture of the Messiah (Christ) in the Old Testament is that portrayed in the Servant Songs of Isaiah. Surely the accomplishments of the Servant in the Songs could only be true of the work of the Messiah, not Isaiah or Israel or anyone else. That fact alone makes this study especially rewarding and enriching.

The treatment of these great passages by my good friend and former colleague is balanced, thorough, and well reasoned. His work is definitely one of the finest studies of Isaiah's Servant Songs in print today.

Now let us be thankful for all that this Servant suffered and accomplished for us. And let us learn from that Servant. Although we cannot emulate His atoning death (Isa. 53:5, 7-12), except in the sense of Luke 9:23-24, we can—indeed, we are exhorted to—emulate His servant attitude and His other servant actions (Isa. 50:10; John 13:4-17; Phil. 2:1-18).

KENNETH L. BARKER

Preface

Isaiah's Servant Songs (42:1-9; 49:1-13; 50:4-11; 52:13—53:12) have been among the most controversial passages in the Old Testament. The theological significance of the Servant Songs is reflected in the traditional view of conservative Christian scholars that the Servant of whom they speak is none other than Jesus the Messiah (cf. Acts 8:26-39). For example, August Pieper has asserted, "For all Christian exegetes the Messianic interpretation is *a priori* the correct one because of the precedent set by the New Testament writers."[1]

This study in the Servant Songs is written out of the conviction that the Lord Jesus Christ is indeed the Servant of whom they speak. Various evidences in support of the messianic view will be mentioned in the exposition and summarized in the concluding chapter. I assume the inspiration and inerrancy of Scripture, the unity of the sixty-six chapters of Isaiah, and the reality of predictive prophecy. It is my conclusion that all four

---

1. August Pieper, *Isaiah II: An Exposition of Isaiah 40-66* (1919; trans., Milwaukee: Northwestern, 1979), p. 177. For other solutions to the identity of the Servant, see pages 9-17.

Servant passages are directly messianic in their portrayal of the Servant. That does not exclude the possibility that Isaiah's contemporaries and the later generation of Jews in Babylonian captivity may have expected an imminent deliverance by the Servant.

The Servant poems will be interpreted within the framework of a premillennial interpretation of prophecy. Attention will be given in the exposition to such matters as the position and role of the Servant, the relationship of the Servant in the Songs to the prophecies of the Davidic Messiah, and the time of the fulfillment of the Servant's task.

This volume is written as an introduction to the problems and literature relating to the Servant Songs. It is hoped that pastors and Bible students will find herein a doorway for further study and exposition of the delightful prophecies of Isaiah. However, my purpose will not be accomplished if the reader is not drawn to faith in and worship of the Servant, whose pathway of suffering and death led Him to glorious exaltation at Yahweh's right hand, awaiting the time when He will come again to establish a right order on all the earth.

The divine name *YHWH* (commonly called the Tetragrammaton) has been transliterated as *Yahweh* in this commentary. Most English versions (including the NIV, the text used in this commentary) translate this divine name as LORD (the ASV translated it "Jehovah"). It is the personal covenant name of God by which He revealed Himself to Israel.

I would like to give a personal word of thanks to a number of persons without whose assistance and encouragement this volume would never have been completed: to Dr. Kenneth L. Barker and Dr. Roy B. Zuck, who read the original drafts and offered much helpful assistance; to my understanding wife Barbara, who not only endured the idiosyncrasies of an author-husband but also employed her proofreading skills at numerous stages of the process; to numerous students and colleagues who have encouraged the publication of the project in this current format; and to the editorial staff of Moody Press, for undertaking the publication of this volume.

1
Introduction

The word *servant* (עֶבֶד, *'ebed*) occurs twenty times in Isaiah 40–53. In each instance it is clear that Yahweh (יְהוָה, "the LORD") is the Sovereign whom "the servant" represents.[1] Eight of the occurrences are found in the four passages commonly designated as the Servant Songs.

THE SERVANT OF YAHWEH

The word *'ebed* can refer to a slave (Ex. 21:20–21) or a vassal king (2 Sam. 10:19), an individual subject (Gen. 21:25)

---

1. In contrast to Isaiah 54–66 where it is used eleven times and only in the plural ("My servants," 54:17; 56:6; 63:17; 65:8, 9, 13 [thrice], 14, 15; 66:14), *'ebed* occurs only in the singular in Isaiah 41–53, where it refers to the prophet Isaiah once (44:26), to Jacob/Israel eleven times outside the Servant Songs (41:8–9; 42:19 [twice]; 43:10; 44:1, 2, 21 [twice]; 45:4; 48:20), and to the figure in the Servant Songs eight times (42:1; 49:3, 5, 6, 7; 50:10; 52:13; 53:11). Also, five out of nine occurrences of *'ebed* in Isaiah 1–39 are in the singular, but show no affinity to those in chaps. 40–53. The complete expression *'ebed yhwh* ("servant of the LORD") occurs only in 42:19, where it refers to Israel.

or a tributary nation (1 Chron. 18:2, 6, 13).[2] In all those cases
the term refers to a person or group characterized by dependence
and servitude. Royal officials and personal representatives of a
king were 'ebedim (Gen. 40:20; 1 Sam. 19:1; 2 Kings 22:12).
The term could indicate a degree of honor, depending on the
position of the one served.[3] To be the "servant of God" or
"servant of Yahweh" denoted the highest honor.

The full expression "the servant of Yahweh" (עֶבֶד יָהְוֶה, 'ebed
yhwh) occurs twenty-two times in the Old Testament. It refers to
Moses seventeen times, Joshua two times, and David two times
(in the superscriptions to Pss. 18 and 36). The final instance
refers to the national servant Israel in Isaiah 42:19. The similar
expression "the servant of God" refers to Moses four times.
More frequent expressions are "his servant" or "my servant,"
with the pronoun referring to God.

Many individuals in the Old Testament were called "servants" of God or Yahweh, particularly those chosen by Him to
accomplish tasks related to His covenant people. Abraham, the
recipient of the Abrahamic covenant, was called Yahweh's "servant" (Gen. 26:24; Ps. 105:6), as were his descendants Isaac
(Gen. 24:14) and Jacob (Ex. 32:13; Ezek. 37:25), to whom the
Abrahamic covenant was reconfirmed. Moses, the mediator of
the Sinaitic covenant, which constituted Israel a vassal nation
under Yahweh, was identified as Yahweh's "servant" (Ex. 14:31;
Num. 12:7; Deut. 34:5; 1 Kings 8:56), as was his successor,
Joshua, who led the people into the land of promise (Josh.
24:29).

Kings, particularly those of the Davidic line, are spoken of
as servants of Yahweh (2 Chron. 32:16; Isa. 22:20; Hag. 2:23).

2. Cf. Colin Brown, ed., *The New International Dictionary of New Testament
Theology* (Grand Rapids: Zondervan, 1975), 3:608; R. Laird Harris,
Gleason L. Archer, Jr., and Bruce K. Waltke, eds., *Theological Wordbook
of the Old Testament* (Chicago: Moody, 1980), 2:639; Gerhard Kittel and
Gerhard Friedrich, eds., *Theological Dictionary of the New Testament*
(Grand Rapids: Eerdmans, 1964–76), 5:654–717 (the same as Walther
Zimmerli and Joachim Jeremias, *The Servant of God*, rev. ed. [London:
SCM, 1965]).
3. The term could also be used by a person as a humble self-designation to
show his deference to a superior (Gen. 33:5; 2 Sam. 9:8; 2 Kings 8:13).

David is frequently referred to as Yahweh's servant (e.g., 1 Kings 11:38; Ps. 89:3; Jer. 33:21-22, 26). One of the functions of the king as Yahweh's servant is indicated in 2 Samuel 3:18: "the LORD promised David, 'By my servant David I will rescue my people Israel . . . from the hand of all their enemies.'"

Yahweh's prophets (1 Kings 18:36; 2 Kings 17:23; Jer. 7:25; Amos 3:7) as well as His priests were designated as His servants (Ps. 134:1). Even the Gentile king Nebuchadnezzar, whom God used to fulfill His purpose for His people, was referred to as His servant (Jer. 25:9; 27:6; 43:10). Yahweh considered all those who worship Him to be His servants (e.g., Isa. 56:6). Even the angels of God are His servants (Ps. 103:20-21).

THE SERVANT SONGS

The German scholar Bernhard Duhm specified four passages (Isa. 42:1-4; 49:1-6; 50:4-9; 52:13—53:12) that he said should be isolated from their context because they were written by an author a century later than the author he called Deutero-Isaiah.[4] Those four passages have become known as "the Servant Songs." However, the term is merely "a scholarly convention,"[5] and does not correctly identify the literary genre of the passages according to more recent form-critical terminology. The literary genre of each song will be discussed in the exposition of the individual passages.

In contrast with Duhm's isolation of the Songs from their literary context, the consensus of contemporary scholarship has recognized that the passages are an integral part of their context.[6] But scholars continue to disagree about the extent of each Servant passage,[7] the meaning of each song, the contribution of each to the message of the prophet, and the overall significance of the

---

4. Bernhard Duhm, *Das Buch Jesaia übersetzt und erklärt* (Göttingen, 1892), pp. xviii, 204ff., 365ff.
5. Roy F. Melugin, *The Formation of Isaiah 40-55* (New York: Walter de Gruyter, 1976), p. 64.
6. E.g., Walther Zimmerli and Joachim Jeremias, "*pais theou*," in Kittel, and Friedrich, *Theological Dictionary of the New Testament*, 5:654-717.
7. Harold H. Rowley, *The Servant of the Lord and Other Essays on the Old Testament*, 2d ed. (Oxford: Basil Blackwell, 1952), p. 6, n. 1.

Servant Songs. Also, some scholars add Isaiah 61:1–3 to the list
of the Servant Songs.[8]

NEW TESTAMENT INTERPRETATION: JESUS IS THE SERVANT

THE SERVANT AS UNDERSTOOD BY JESUS

Jesus summarized His mission by affirming that "even the
Son of Man did not come to be served, but to serve, and to give
his life as a ransom for many" (Mark 10:45). His consciousness
of His coming suffering and death was recorded frequently by
the gospel writers (e.g., Matt. 16:21; 17:22–23; 20:17–19; 26:12,
28, 31). What was the source of Jesus' expectation of His suffering and death? Some scholars have found the Old Testament
source in Daniel 7 rather than Isaiah 53.[9] However, R. T. France
has refuted that view and has demonstrated that Jesus viewed His
vicarious and redemptive death for sinners as a fulfillment of the
mission of the Servant in Isaiah 53.[10]

Jesus' single formal quotation from Isaiah 53 occurred on
the night before the crucifixion when He told His disciples, "It is
written: 'And he was numbered with the transgressors'; and I tell
you that this must be fulfilled in me. Yes, what is written about
me is reaching its fulfillment" (Luke 22:37, citing Isa. 53:12).
France has shown that this quotation is both authentic and
contextually meaningful and that it reflects Jesus' belief that He
was fulfilling the redemptive work of the Servant of Yahweh.

8. R. T. France, *Jesus and the Old Testament: His Application of Old Testament Passages to Himself and His Mission* (Grand Rapids: Baker, 1982),
   pp. 132–35.
9. C. F. D. Moule, *The Phenomenon of the New Testament* (Naperville, Ill.:
   Alec R. Allenson, 1967), p. 96; C. K. Barrett, "The Background of Mark
   10:45," in *New Testament Essays: Studies in Memory of T. W. Manson*, ed.
   Angus J. B. Higgins (Manchester: Manchester U., 1959), pp. 1–18;
   Morna D. Hooker, *Jesus and the Servant* (London: S.P.C.K., 1959),
   p. 155.
10. France, *Jesus and the Old Testament.* The following summary review of
    the evidence is based on France's discussion, pp. 114–32. France's treat-
    ment of Isaiah 61:1–3 as cited or alluded to in Luke 4:17–21; Matt. 5:3–
    4; 11:5 further supports the identification of Jesus with the Servant
    (pp. 132–35).

That Jesus quoted at all from Isaiah 53 on the eve of His death indicates that He saw His death in the light of that chapter. His quotation of the passage from Isaiah (which is immediately followed by the words "he bore the sin of many, and made intercession for the transgressors") strongly implies He had in mind the redemptive nature of His death. The strong fulfillment formula used by Jesus in Luke 22:37 further confirms His self-identification with the Servant of Yahweh spoken of in Isaiah 53.[11]

Two clear allusions to Isaiah 53 are found in Jesus' teaching: Mark 10:45 (cf. Matt. 20:28) and Mark 14:24 (cf. Matt. 26:28; Luke 22:20). Mark 10:45 states, "For even the Son of Man did not come to be served, but to serve, and to give his life as a ransom for many." France refutes the view that rejects the authenticity of this saying. Although a linguistic connection between διακονῆσαι (diakonēsai, "to serve") and עֶבֶד ('ebed, "servant") cannot be demonstrated,[12] France does demonstrate that there is a close connection in thought and suggests that Jesus' Aramaic word behind the Greek word may have echoed 'ebed.[13]

The phrase "to give his life as a ransom for many" alludes to Isaiah 53:10, "though the LORD makes his life a guilt offering." Although λύτρον (lutron, "ransom") does not occur in the LXX of Isaiah 53, and never translates אָשָׁם ('āshām, "guilt offering"), yet in Jesus' statement lutron is a free translation of 'āshām for the concept of substitution present in "ransom" is also found in "guilt offering" (cf. Lev. 5:17–19, where the 'āshām is distinct from the "restitution" of 5:16; 6:4–5). Further, the work of the Servant in Isaiah 53 is one of substitution, forming the background for the significance of "guilt offering" in 53:10. Apart from the question of literary allusion, Jesus' statement in Mark 10:45 is "a perfect summary of the central theme of Isaiah 53, that of a vicarious and redeeming death." Thus Jesus was deliberately claiming the role of the Servant as His own.[14]

The second clear allusion to a Servant song is found in

11. Ibid., pp. 114–16.
12. Contrary to Jeremias ("pais theou," 5:712), who dogmatically affirms such a connection.
13. France, Jesus and the Old Testament, pp. 114–18.
14. Ibid., pp. 119–20.

Mark 14:24: "This is my blood of the covenant, which is poured out for many." Although "the covenant" referred to here may relate to that promised in Jeremiah 31:31, it is noteworthy that the Servant in Isaiah's Servant Songs is twice referred to as "a covenant for the people" (Isa. 42:6; 49:8). But the words "poured out for many" allude to Isaiah 53:12, "he poured out his life unto death" and "bore the sin of many" (cf. Isa. 53:11, "my righteous servant will justify many"). Jesus couched the statement regarding His vicarious and redemptive suffering in words reminiscent of Isaiah 53 and its central theme.[15]

Thus an open-minded consideration of the passages noted above leads to France's conclusion that "Jesus saw his mission as that of the Servant of Yahweh, that he predicted that in fulfillment of that role he must suffer and die, and that he regarded his suffering and death as, like that of the Servant, vicarious and redemptive."[16]

THE SERVANT AS PREACHED BY THE APOSTLES

Following the death and resurrection of Jesus Christ, the earliest testimony to His person and work linked Him with Isaiah's Servant. Thus Oscar Cullmann affirms: "*The Acts of the Apostles* offers us the strongest proof of the fact that in the most ancient period of early Christianity there existed an explanation of the person and work of Jesus which we could characterize somewhat inaccurately as an *ebed Yahweh* Christology—or more exactly as a 'Paidology.'"[17] The term "Paidology" is derived from the Greek παῖς (*pais*), which is a broad word of relationship meaning "servant" or "son." The contextual associations in the four passages noted below indicate the meaning of "servant."

---

15. France treats three additional passages (Matt. 3:15; Mark 9:12; Luke 11:22) in which Jesus' words are possible allusions to Isaiah 53 (pp. 123–25).
16. Ibid., p. 132.
17. Oscar Cullmann, *The Christology of the New Testament* (Philadelphia: Westminster, 1959), p. 73. For a contrary opinion, see Donald L. Jones, "The Title 'Servant' in Luke-Acts," in *Luke-Acts: New Perspectives from the Society of Biblical Literature Seminar*, ed. Charles H. Talbert (New York: Crossroad, 1984), pp. 148–65.

The title παῖς τοῦ θεοῦ (*pais tou theou,* "servant of God"), which is the LXX translation of Isaiah's עֶבֶד יַהְוֶה (*'ebed yhwh,* "servant of Yahweh"), is ascribed to Jesus four times in Acts (and only in chaps. 3 and 4).

In Acts 3:13 Peter alludes to Isaiah 52:13 when he says, "The God of Abraham, Isaac and Jacob, the God of our fathers, has glorified his servant Jesus. You handed him over to be killed." Later in the same sermon Peter simply refers to Jesus under the Christological title of Servant: "When God raised up his servant . . . " (Acts 3:26). A day or so later, the following prayer of the Christian community probably reflected terminology from Peter's teaching: "Indeed Herod and Pontius Pilate met together with the Gentiles and the people of Israel in this city to conspire against your holy servant Jesus, whom you anointed" (Acts 4:27; cf. v. 30).

Based partially on those early Christological statements, Cullmann conjectures that the Servant of Yahweh concept dominated the Christology of the apostle Peter.[18] That is confirmed by 1 Peter 2:21–25, which includes a direct quotation from Isaiah 53:9 and numerous allusions to Isaiah 53.

Although the apostle Paul uses Isaiah 53 less than might be expected in view of his emphasis on the substitutionary death of Christ, and although he does not use the term *pais* of Jesus, there are clear references to Isaiah 53 and its concepts in Paul's teaching. In Christological statements, Paul alludes to Isaiah 53:6 (in 2 Cor. 5:21), Isaiah 53:11 (in Rom. 5:19), and Isaiah 53:12 (in Rom. 4:25). (The citations in Romans 10:16 and 15:21 refer to Paul's own missionary preaching, not to the work of the Servant.) Despite the limited number of quotations from Isaiah 53 and the absence of the title *pais,* Paul's theology clearly stresses the concept of vicarious and substitutionary atonement (Rom. 5:12–21; 1 Cor. 15:3; Phil. 2:7; etc.). The absence of a more direct emphasis on Jesus' title of Servant is probably because of the centrality Paul gives to the title Lord (κύριος, *kurios*), which stresses His exaltation at the right hand of God. The concept of exaltation is,

18. Cullmann, *Christology,* pp. 74–75.

of course, affirmed in the Servant Songs (Isa. 52:13, 15; 53:10–12) but is not developed there in detail.

A comment needs to be added concerning the Christology of the gospel writers themselves. Matthew 8:16–17 cites Isaiah 53:4 as fulfilled in Jesus. Matthew understood the taking away of disease by the Servant as an anticipation of the work to be accomplished through His death. In Matthew 12:18–21 the evangelist cites Isaiah 42:1–4 (the first Servant song) but only in regard to the peripheral point that Jesus forbade public testimony of His healing ministry. It is interesting that Matthew, who quotes so much from the Old Testament, makes no reference to the suffering Servant of Isaiah 53 in his Passion narrative.

Although Mark (except for the teaching of Jesus that he records) makes no reference to the Servant of Yahweh or the Servant Songs, he nevertheless seems to view Jesus as a Servant through much of his gospel. It is possible that that was because of the influence of Peter, for whom the Servant Christology was central. Likewise, Luke makes no reference to the Servant theme in his gospel apart from Jesus' own teaching.

In recording the testimony of John the Baptist, the apostle John alludes clearly to Isaiah 53: "Look, the Lamb of God, who takes away the sin of the world!" (John 1:29; cf. v. 36). Some scholars have suggested that an Aramaic phrase meaning both "Lamb of God" and "Servant of God" probably lies behind the Greek expression ἀμνὸς τοῦ θεοῦ (amnos tou theou). Cullmann has concluded, "Since the expression 'Lamb of God' is not commonly used in the Old Testament as a designation for the paschal lamb, it is probable that the author of John thought primarily of the ebed Yahweh."[19] Other allusions to the Servant Songs found in John's gospel are in the narrative of Jesus' baptism (John 1:23–34) and in John 12:38 (citing Isa. 53:1).

It may be concluded, therefore, that not only the teaching of Jesus but also the earliest apostolic doctrine clearly affirmed that Jesus' death was substitutionary and redemptive in fulfillment of the Servant of Yahweh passages of Isaiah.

19. Ibid., p. 71.

HISTORICAL VIEWS: THE IDENTITY OF THE SERVANT

The plethora of divergent interpretations concerning the identity of the Servant in Isaiah's Songs can be grouped into three classifications: the individual, the collective, and the cultic.[20] I will summarize and then briefly trace the historical development of those classifications.

CLASSIFICATION OF THE VIEWS

The individual interpretations. These views regard the Servant of Yahweh as a specific person, whether past, present, or future from the perspective of the prophet. Subcategories of this approach include the "autobiographical view" and the "messianic view." Because the Songs "refer to the Servant in the singular and describe the life and experiences of an individual (His birth, obedience, suffering, death, and triumph),"[21] it is natural for readers to assume reference to an individual—as did the Ethiopian in Acts 8:34. The possibility that the Servant is a poetic personification for a group or nation has substance outside the Songs[22] but not in them.

Historical figures with whom the Servant has been identified include Moses, Josiah, Hezekiah, Uzziah, Isaiah, Jeremiah, Ezekiel, Jehoiachin, Cyrus, Zerubbabel (or his son Meshullam), Sheshbazzar, "Deutero-Isaiah," an unknown contemporary of the prophet, and Eleazer (a martyr during the period of the Maccabees). However, the predominant Christian interpretation from New Testament times until the end of the nineteenth century was that the Servant is the Messiah, fulfilled in Jesus of Nazareth.

The collective interpretations. The collective views regard the

---

20. These views have been carefully traced by Christopher R. North, *The Suffering Servant in Deutero-Isaiah: An Historical and Critical Study*, 2d ed. (London: Oxford U., 1956), pp. 6-116; Rowley, *Servant of the Lord*, pp. 4-48; and updated by Colin G. Kruse, "The Servant Songs: Interpretive Trends Since C. R. North," *Studia Biblica et Theologica* 8 (April 1978):3-27.

21. R. T. France, "Servant of the Lord (Yahweh, Jehovah)," in Merrill C. Tenney, ed., *Zondervan Pictorial Encyclopedia of the Bible* (Grand Rapids: Zondervan, 1975), 5:360.

22. Cf. note 1 of this chapter.

Servant as a group personified in individual terms. Subcategories of this classification regard the Servant as: (1) empirical Israel, that is, the entire Jewish people; (2) ideal Israel (e.g., "the ideal impersonation of the theocratic attributes of the nation");[23] (3) a righteous remnant within the nation Israel; (4) the Davidic dynasty; (5) the prophetic order; (6) the priestly order; or (7) some combination of the above.

Because the passages surrounding the Servant Songs refer to national Israel as the Servant eleven times,[24] it appears natural to conclude that the Servant in the Songs may also be a personification for national Israel. Further, the Servant in the Songs is described in language closely corresponding to that applied to the Servant Israel outside the Songs (e.g., "my chosen" [42:1; cf. 41:8-9], "my servant" [42:1; 49:3; cf. 44:21], "whom I uphold" [42:1; cf. 41:10], "I called you" [42:6; 49:1; cf. 41:9]). He is also explicitly addressed as Israel in 49:3.[25]

However, a major obstacle encountered by the empirical Israel view is that the Servant cannot be Israel because He has a ministry to Israel (49:5-6; cf. 53:8). That problem has led many scholars to opt for one of the other subcategories of the collective view, or to adopt one of the individual views.

The mythological or cultic interpretations. Some interpreters, particularly those associated with the Scandinavian myth-and-ritual school, see the Servant as a mythological symbol growing out of a cultic ceremony involving the symbolic death and resurrection of the king, a ceremony supposedly based on the Babylonian myth of the dying and rising god Tammuz.[26]

The synthetic interpretations. France is probably correct when he says,

> Few scholars today hold to an exclusively collective or an exclusively individual interpretation. Some would see a progression of thought from the collective figure of the earlier Servant Songs to a

23. S. R. Driver, Isaiah: His Life and Times (New York: Anson D. F. Randolph, n.d.), p. 179.
24. See note 1 of this chapter.
25. See commentary in chapter 3 on 49:3.
26. See North, Suffering Servant, pp. 220-39; cf. pp. 69-71; 101-3; cf. Rowley, Servant of the Lord, pp. 42-48.

more fully individualized figure in the fourth. The ideal for Israel was summed up in an ideal individual—the Messiah.[27]

H. Wheeler Robinson's view of "corporate personality,"[28] which suggests that the Servant can both act for Israel and sum up Israel in Himself, has been particularly influential in this trend. The concept is accepted by numerous scholars of varying theological viewpoints and methodological approaches.[29]

THE HISTORICAL DEVELOPMENT OF THE VIEWS

Pre-Christian views. Little evidence exists concerning the Jewish interpretation of the Servant in pre-Christian times. In Isaiah 42:1 the LXX identifies the Servant as Jacob/Israel. The Wisdom of Solomon (2:3; 5:1-7) may have identified the Servant with those who are righteous. The author of the Parables of Enoch apparently identified the Servant with the messianic Son of Man.[30] The Jewish-oriented Nunc Dimittis in Luke 2:29-32 clearly interprets Isaiah 49:6 in messianic terms.

New Testament interpretation. It was concluded above that not only the teaching of Jesus but also the earliest apostolic doctrine clearly affirmed that Jesus' sufferings culminated in a substitutionary and redemptive death in fulfillment of the Servant Songs. Thus the New Testament clearly affirms the messianic interpretation of the Servant. It is noteworthy that the messianic view continued as the unanimous Christian view until the end of the eighteenth century.

Jewish interpretations after New Testament times. Because individual scholars (Jewish and Christian) have not consistently identified the Servant in the earlier Servant songs with the figure of the Servant in Isaiah 52:13—53:12, this historical summary

27. France, "Servant of the Lord" 5:360.
28. H. Wheeler Robinson, *The Cross in the Old Testament: A Study in Deutero-Isaiah* (Philadelphia: Westminster, 1955); *Corporate Personality in Ancient Israel* (Philadelphia: Fortress, 1967).
29. E.g., North, *Suffering Servant*; Rowley, *Servant of the Lord*, pp. 1–88; France, "Servant of the Lord," 5:360.
30. See references to Enoch cited by North, *Suffering Servant*, pp. 7–8.

of Jewish and Christian views relates particularly to the identity of the Servant in the fourth Servant song. The growing Jewish tradition from the first century A.D. to medieval times favored some form of the individual messianic interpretation (or the related concept of two Messiahs). The Targum of Jonathan ben Uzziel (which seems to reflect the earliest Jewish views during the Christian era) identifies the Servant as the Messiah in the first and last songs, though it transfers the sufferings in the last song to Israel or the Gentiles. The developing Jewish view gradually allowed for the concept of a suffering Messiah but characteristically disallowed those sufferings to culminate in a violent death followed by a resurrection. Some Jews distinguished between two Messiahs: Messiah ben David, who suffers but does not die (sometimes associated with the Servant); and Messiah ben Joseph, who is slain, but with no preceding sufferings.[31] Varying forms of the messianic view have been held by some Jewish scholars down to modern times.

However, the collective interpretation became the dominant Jewish view from the time it was introduced by medieval Jewish commentators. Except for a reference in Origen ascribing the "righteous remnant view" to certain Jews, there is little evidence for the collective interpretation before Rashi (d. 1105) and the twelfth-century Jewish commentators. From the twelfth century to the middle of the twentieth century, the Jewish collective view has oscillated between the empirical Israel view and the righteous remnant view.[32] However, several recent Jewish scholars have identified the Servant with a historical individual.[33]

A few of the modern individual interpretations were already anticipated by Jewish writers who viewed the Servant as Jeremiah, Josiah, Hezekiah, Job, or Nehemiah. Christopher R. North

31. North, *Suffering Servant*, pp. 11–12, 16–17.
32. Ibid., pp. 17–20.
33. Julian Morgenstern, "The Suffering Servant—a New Solution," *Vetus Testamentum* 11 (1961):425–31 (the Servant was perhaps a son of Zerubbabel); Harry M. Orlinsky, "The So-called 'Servant of the Lord' and 'Suffering Servant' in Second Isaiah," in *Studies on the Second Part of the Book of Isaiah*, Supplements to *Vetus Testamentum* 14 (Leiden: E. J. Brill, 1967), pp. 17–51 (the Servant was "Deutero-Isaiah").

concludes: "It is evident that the Jews themselves have been almost as perplexed about the Servant as Christians have been ever since, a century and a half ago, they [numerous Christian scholars] abandoned the Messianic interpretation."[34]

Christian interpretations. The messianic interpretation was held unanimously[35] by Christian writers until late in the eighteenth century, when the introduction of the "Deutero-Isaiah" view (and its corollary, the dissolution of predictive prophecy in the Servant Songs) gave rise to alternate views of the Servant.

In the third edition of his commentary on Isaiah (1789), Johann Christoph Döderlein gave up the messianic interpretation for the collective view that identified the Servant as the entire nation Israel. Already suggested by Heinrich Stephani in 1787, that view followed the denial of the Isaianic authorship of Isaiah 40–66 by J. S. Semler (1771-75). The Christian trend toward identifying the Servant as a historical individual also began about this time (cf. Karl Friedrich Bahrdt's nomination of Hezekiah in 1780).[36]

The view that the Servant was the ideal Israel was advocated by J. C. Eckermann in 1794. When Samuel Davidson adopted that view in 1863, he was the first English scholar to abandon the messianic interpretation.[37] Other English scholars opting for the view included T. K. Cheyne (1870), A. B. Davidson (1884), and S. R. Driver (1888). It is sometimes difficult to distinguish between the ideal Israel view and the righteous remnant view, first advocated by H. E. G. Paulus in 1792. In 1799 E. F. K. Rosenmüller identified the Servant as the order of the prophets, while an anonymous German author (1801) suggested the priestly order.

Two high-water marks in the history of the study of the Servant Songs relate to Bernhard Duhm (1892) and Sigmund

---

34. North, *Suffering Servant*, p. 21.
35. The one exception was the view of Grotius, who identified the Servant as Jeremiah (ibid., p. 27).
36. North, *Suffering Servant*, pp. 27-28, 39-40; North traces the other historical views before (pp. 40-42) and after Duhm (pp. 47-57); cf. Rowley, *Servant of the Lord*, pp. 33-41.
37. North, *Suffering Servant*, p. 33.

Mowinckel (1921). Duhm viewed the Servant as an unknown teacher of the law. But more significant than his own identification of the Servant was his critique of the collective view, which (for the most part) sounded its death knell and inaugurated a spate of individual interpretations: Eleazar (2 Macc. 6:18–31, Alfred Bertholet, 1899), Zerubbabel (Ernst Sellin, 1898), Jehoiachin (Sellin, 1901), Moses (Sellin [!], 1922), Deutero-Isaiah (Sellin [!!], 1930), Ezekiel (R. Kraetzschmar, 1900), Cyrus (T. H. Weir, 1908). A few scholars did continue to hold the collective view (Karl Budde, 1900; F. W. K. Giesebrecht, 1902; Arthur Samuel Peake, 1904), the righteous remnant view (E. König, 1898), or the ideal Israel view (J. Skinner, 1898).[38]

The "historico-messianic view"—that the Servant was an anonymous contemporary whom Deutero-Isaiah believed to be the Messiah—was advocated by Rudolph Kittel (1898), Wilhelm Rudolph (1925), and W. O. E. Oesterley (1930).[39]

The "autobiographical view"—that the Servant was Deutero-Isaiah himself—was originated by Sigmund Mowinckel in 1921 and has been very influential to the present day.[40] Mowinckel was followed by Hermann Gunkel (1921, 1929) and Joachim Begrich (1938). Ernst Sellin (1930) and Karl Elliger (1933) also followed this view but attributed the fourth song to "Trito-Isaiah," who wrote about the sufferings of Deutero-Isaiah. The decline of the collective view that equates the Servant with Israel has been even more prominent since the middle of the twentieth century.[41] R. N. Whybray has more recently defended the "autobiographical view." He affirms that the Servant was Deutero-Isaiah and denies that his sufferings were vicarious or fatal.[42]

The "corporate personality" concept associated with H. Wheeler Robinson (1934) tried to harmonize the apparently

38. Ibid., pp. 49–57; cf. Rowley, *Servant of the Lord*, pp. 12–19.
39. North, *Suffering Servant*, pp. 85–88.
40. Ibid., pp. 72–85; cf. Rowley, *Servant of the Lord*, pp. 7–12.
41. Cf. Kruse, "The Servant Songs," p. 24.
42. R. N. Whybray, *Thanksgiving for a Liberated Prophet: An Interpretation of Isaiah Chapter 53* (Sheffield: Journal for the Study of the Old Testament, 1978).

contradictory features of the corporate servant and the individual servant. According to this view the group can function as a continuing entity in a single representative individual of the group. Thus Isaiah's portrait of the servant is seen to progress from the group to the individual (North) or to oscillate between the group and the individual (Harold H. Rowley).

In 1942 H. S. Nyberg synthesized the concepts of the Tammuz-mystery, the kingship ideology (regarding the role of the king in the new year's cult drama), and the ancestor ideology (somewhat akin to Robinson's "corporate personality"). He was followed by Ivan Engnell (1945) who saw the Servant as the future Messiah who was depicted in the myth-and-ritual categories of the preexilic kings (found particularly in the royal psalms). Somewhat similar views were advocated by Helmer Ringgren (1954). Aage Bentzen (1948) conceived of the Servant figure in prophetic categories with Moses as a model.[43]

Building on the view of Engnell, John H. Eaton agreed that the whole cycle of Deutero-Isaiah (Isa. 40–55) was modeled on the ideas of the autumn New Year festival, which included the royal figure's calling, ritual suffering, and glorification. Eaton argued (1976) that the bulk of the psalms of the individual should be interpreted as royal psalms, a number of which were composed for the autumnal ritual (e.g., Pss. 22, 23, 51, 75, 91, 118, 121). Eaton enlarged the royal psalmody and also reexamined the autumnal festival and concluded that "the festal presentation of God's supremacy and kingship had indeed been combined with a presentation of the royal office as the chosen organ of that kingship, and that the glorification of the king in the grace of Yahweh was preceded by his symbolic humiliation to the verge of death." On this foundation Eaton later proposed (1979) that the main ideas and dramatic form of Isaiah 40–55 were determined by the same tradition reflected in the royal psalms.[44]

After reviewing eighteen views of the Servant Songs (pub-

43. North, *Suffering Servant*, pp. 223–39.
44. John H. Eaton, *Kingship in the Psalms* (London: SCM, 1976); *Festal Drama in Deutero-Isaiah* (London: S.P.C.K., 1979), pp. 6–7.

lished from about 1950 to 1975), Colin G. Kruse summarizes
recent trends: (1) the four Servant Songs are now regarded as a
literary unity with the rest of Deutero-Isaiah, in contrast to the
fragmentary view of Duhm; (2) the once predominant identification of the Servant as Israel has been almost universally abandoned; (3) very few scholars continue to identify the Servant
with some historic person; (4) some scholars still think the Near
Eastern ritual myths have influenced the Servant Songs, in spite
of the demonstration by Josef Scharbert that the parallels are
superficial rather than essential;[45] (5) some scholars view the
evident anonymity of the Servant as intentional; and (6) several
scholars maintain that the Servant idea transcends its historical
context and points to the future.[46]

Throughout this labyrinth of interpretive history, evangelical
scholars have continued to maintain the messianic interpretation
of the Servant. Their views will be referred to at appropriate
places in the following chapters.

SUMMARY OF HISTORICAL VIEWS

The messianic interpretation of the Servant, as taught by
Jesus and the apostles, was the unanimous Christian view until
the end of the eighteenth century. Likewise, some form of the
messianic interpretation was the predominant Jewish interpretation until the Middle Ages, when the great medieval Jewish
commentators introduced the collective interpretation (either
empirical Israel or the righteous remnant).

The invention of Deutero-Isaiah at the end of the eighteenth
century was accompanied by a rejection of predictive prophecy
and led to the abandonment of the messianic view by numerous
critical scholars, who then adopted the various Jewish views,
particularly the collective views. Duhm's introduction of Trito-
Isaiah in 1892 sent the collective interpretation into near eclipse
and stimulated the growth of the individual interpretations. The

45. Josef Scharbert, "Stellvertretendes Sühnleiden in dem Ebed-Yahwe-Lied-
    ern und in altorientalischen Ritual Texten," *Biblische Zeitschrift* 2
    (1958):190–213.
46. Kruse, "The Servant Songs," pp. 23–25.

individual views reached their *reductio ad absurdem* in Sellin, who was in turn certain of four different individual interpretations. The twentieth century has seen the refinement of the cultic view, but adherents of the autobiographical view (first introduced by Mowinckel in 1921), along with a number of advocates of the corporate or fluid viewpoints, are still the leading competitors of the messianic view as held by evangelical scholars.

THE CONTEXT OF THE SONGS OF THE SERVANT

THE HISTORICAL CONTEXT

Isaiah the prophet ministered "during the reigns of Uzziah, Jotham, Ahaz and Hezekiah, kings of Judah" (Isa. 1:1). His active ministry covered a period of over forty years, from at least 739 B.C. ("the year that King Uzziah died," 6:1) to after 701 B.C. (the invasion of Sennacherib, 36:1). Yet Isaiah was apparently still living in 681 B.C. to record the death of Sennacherib (37:38). Thus his life extended into the reign of Manasseh, at which time, according to Hebrew tradition, he suffered martyrdom by being sawed asunder (cf. Heb. 11:37).

Isaiah thus began his ministry at a time of political, military, and economic prosperity for both Judah and Israel (cf. 2 Kings 14:25, 28; 2 Chron. 26). That prosperity produced a spirit of self-confidence and self-indulgence that resulted in oppression, injustice, foreign alliances, and religious hypocrisy. Those sins were denounced by Isaiah, who predicted the overthrow of Israel at the hands of Assyria (e.g., Isa. 28:1–13) and of Judah and Jerusalem by Babylon (e.g., 39:1–8).

Isaiah's references to the captivity of Judah in Babylon (which happened over a century after Isaiah's ministry ended) have created problems for many Bible scholars. Isaiah's prophecies in chapters 1–39 are addressed to Judah, Israel, and Gentile nations in the eighth century B.C., but the prophecies of chapters 40–66 refer for the most part to the time of Judah's exile in Babylon. Consequently, many rationalistic critical scholars (since Döderlein's commentary in 1775) have denied the Isaianic authorship of chapters 40–66 and have ascribed the second portion

Isaiah," during the Babylonian Exile. In 1892 Duhm questioned the unity of chapters 40–66 and ascribed chapters 56–66 to another unknown author in Palestine ("Trito-Isaiah"). The further development of those fragmenting views and the argumentation against the unity of the book of Isaiah can be surveyed in most Old Testament introductions.[47]

I accept the unity of the book of Isaiah as defended by evangelical scholars such as Oswald T. Allis and Edward J. Young.[48] But how can chapters 40–66, with their apparent setting near the end of the Babylonian Exile, be the product of an eighth-century prophet? The essential answer to that question is given by the prophet Amos: "Surely the Sovereign LORD does nothing without revealing his plan to his servants the prophets" (Amos 3:7). The opposite presupposition, that God does not (or cannot) reveal details of future events, was a major factor in the denial of Isaiah's authorship of chapters 40–66. The testimony of the apostle John affirms that authorship (John 1:23; 12:38).

Assuming then that Isaiah 40–66 was not written by a later prophet of the Exile, but rather by Isaiah of Jerusalem in the eighth century B.C. with a prophetic perspective on the future Exile, what relevance (if any) did his message of comfort and hope (chaps. 40–66) have for Judah and Israel of Isaiah's day? Facing the divine judgments on their sins (as announced by Isaiah), which led to the invasion of Sennacherib in 701 B.C., the Israelites of the northern kingdom should have realized the righteousness of King Yahweh, who was bringing to fulfillment the curses of the Sinaitic covenant for their covenant-breaking idolatry (Deut. 28:15–68). They should have become very much aware of their failure to respond in repentance to the proffered restoration aimed at by divine judgment. They also should have

47. E.g., R. K. Harrison, *Introduction to the Old Testament* (Grand Rapids: Eerdmans, 1969), pp. 764–95; Gleason L. Archer, Jr., *A Survey of Old Testament Introduction* (Chicago: Moody, 1964), pp. 329–51; Otto Eissfeldt, *The Old Testament: An Introduction*, trans. Peter R. Ackroyd (London: Basil Blackwell, 1965), pp. 303–46.
48. Oswald T. Allis, *The Unity of Isaiah* (Philadelphia: Presbyterian and Reformed, 1950); Edward J. Young, *Who Wrote Isaiah?* (Grand Rapids: Eerdmans, 1958); cf. Hobart E. Freeman, *An Introduction to the Old Testament Prophets* (Chicago: Moody, 1968), pp. 196–203.

restoration aimed at by divine judgment. They also should have recognized the sovereign rule of Yahweh, who would still fulfill His covenant promises of ultimate blessing for His people in spite of their refusal to participate in them.

More pointedly, the inhabitants of Judah should have recognized that whatever consequences might eventuate from the impending threat of Assyria and the rising threat of Babylon, Yahweh would deliver survivors from the places of exile and fulfill His covenanted promises of blessing in the land of Israel. Ultimate blessing in the distant future meant the survival of some in the immediate future. Moreover, it meant that Yahweh was not wholly casting them off but would be faithful to His covenants to Abraham and David in spite of the present need for judgment on their sins. Of course, Isaiah and his contemporaries could not clearly distinguish between Isaiah's superimposed picture of deliverance from Babylonian Exile and final deliverance from worldwide dispersion by Yahweh's Servant-Messiah.

THE LITERARY CONTEXT

The apparent diversity of two central themes of Isaiah—judgment (chaps. 1–39)[49] and comfort (chaps. 40–66) seems to accommodate those who divide the authorship of the book. However, Yahweh's judgment (emphasized in chaps. 1–39) is a part of His ultimate restoration of the created order (emphasized in chaps. 40–66). Thus the statement of Isaiah's theme as the "salvation of Yahweh through His Servant to the ends of the earth"[50] gives due recognition to the overarching thematic unity of the book. The Servant Songs make a large contribution to that central theme by emphasizing the Servant's ultimate accomplishment of His mission not only to restore the nation Israel to

49. Actually, chapters 36–39 are transitional in the structure of Isaiah. The Assyrian threat is emphasized in chapters 36–37, reminiscent of the first thirty-five chapters of the book, whereas the Babylonian Exile is predicted in 39:5–7, anticipating the rest of the book.
50. Alfred Martin and John A. Martin, *Isaiah: The Glory of the Messiah* (Chicago: Moody, 1983), pp. 173–76.

the land (49:8-12) but also to establish *mishpāṭ* (a just order) on the whole earth (42:1, 3, 4; 49:6).

The emphasis on judgment in the first part of the book (chaps. 1-39) is not total; the future age of salvation is also portrayed there with some prominence (see chaps. 7-12 and 25-27).[51] In chapters 40-66, Yahweh reveals His purpose to save His people both in the immediate future (e.g., in the Cyrus oracle, chap. 45) and also in the more distant future (e.g., the Servant Songs), thus ultimately bringing about the salvation portrayed in the first part of Isaiah.

The Servant Songs have a distinctive theme because they focus attention on an individual Servant, who is distinguished from the national servant in the surrounding chapters. Yet the Servant passages are interwoven with their context and contribute to the development of Isaiah's argument, which parallels and contrasts the long-range prophecies of deliverance by the individual Servant with the nearer deliverance by Cyrus. More detailed attention will be given to contextual relations and literary genres of the individual Servant Songs in the commentary in the following chapters.

THE THEOLOGICAL CONTEXT

A detailed study of the message of Isaiah from the approach of biblical theology results in a virtual synthesis of Old Testament theology. However, such a study is outside the scope of this introductory chapter. Some brief observations on Isaiah's key concepts must suffice.

Isaiah's doctrine of God. In developing the theme of his book,

51. Salvation appears brightly against the black backdrop of judgment (cf. chaps. 7-12; 25-27). Robert B. Chisholm has shown that a large majority of the judgment genre units appears in chapters1-39 (thirty-two out of thirty-eight judgment speeches, all twelve woe oracles, and two of the three condemnatory lawsuits). In terms of literary genre, although twenty-four out of Isaiah's thirty-six salvation announcements and six of his eight salvation oracles are present in chapters 40-66, yet twelve of the fifteen portrayals of salvation are found in chapters 1-39. ("Toward a Form Critical/Structural Analysis of Isaiah" [student paper, Dallas Theological Seminary, 1980], p. 87.)

Isaiah sets forth Yahweh as the King of Israel,[52] who is the sovereign initiator of the judgment and restoration of Israel and of all things. Many individuals, of course, will experience only the "judgment" and not the "salvation." Within Israel, for example, only Yahweh's chosen remnant will return; the others will be destroyed.

The divine generic name *Elohim/El*, stressing God's sovereign power as the Ruler and Controller of creation and history, is certainly appropriate to the great themes of Isaiah, but it is used by him less than 20 times. On the other hand, Isaiah uses the divine personal name *Yahweh* 421 times—appropriate for a message of judgment and restoration addressed to and centering in His covenant people Israel.

Most of the divine epithets and attributes made prominent by Isaiah focus on Yahweh as King. Not only is the title "King" ascribed to Yahweh (6:5; 33:17, 22; 41:21; 43:15; 44:6), and His future reign affirmed (24:23; 52:7), but also there are many implicit indications of divine rule in Isaiah. They include the Suzerain-vassal motif,[53] the *rîb* or covenant lawsuit of Yahweh,[54] the prophet as royal messenger,[55] and the royal shepherd motif.[56] More explicit is the reference to Yahweh as the divine Warrior[57]

---

52. The concept of Yahweh as Israel's King is common in the Old Testament (e.g., 1 Sam. 12:12; Pss. 93; 95–99; Isa. 33:22; 43:15; Ezek. 20:33) and grows out of Israel's covenantal election and redemption in the Exodus event.

53. Cf. George T. Mendenhall, "Covenant Forms in Israelite Tradition," *Biblical Archeologist* 17 (June 1954): 26–46; Meredith G. Kline, *Treaty of the Great King* (Grand Rapids: Eerdmans, 1963); K. A. Kitchen, *The Bible in Its World* (Downers Grove, Ill.: InterVarsity, 1978), pp. 79–85.

54. Cf. B. Gemser, "The *Rib*- or Controversy-Pattern in Hebrew Mentality," Supplements to *Vetus Testamentum* 3 (Leiden: E. J. Brill, 1955), pp. 120–37; Dennis J. McCarthy, *Old Testament Covenant: A Survey of Current Opinion* (Atlanta: John Knox, 1972), pp. 38–40; Claus Westermann, *Basic Forms of Prophetic Speech* (Philadelphia: Westminster, 1967), pp. 199–201.

55. Cf. James F. Ross, "The Prophet as Yahweh's Messenger," in *Israel's Prophetic Heritage*, ed. Bernhard W. Anderson and Walter Harrelson (New York: Harper & Row, 1962), pp. 98–107.

56. Isaiah 40:11; 49:8–10.

57. Patrick D. Miller, *The Divine Warrior in Early Israel* (Cambridge, Mass.: Harvard U., 1973), pp. 173–74.

through the use of the epithet יְהוָה צְבָאוֹת (*yhwh ṣᵉbāʾôt*), "the LORD Almighty" (NIV) or "the LORD of hosts" (KJV). The Preface to the *New International Version* explains the sense of that Hebrew title: "he who is sovereign over all the 'hosts' (powers) in heaven and on earth, especially over the 'hosts' (armies) of Israel."[58] That this epithet is used fifty-six times in Isaiah 1–39 and only six times in 40–66 is probably due to the function of the warrior as an executor of judgment. One of the functions of kingship in the ancient Near East was that of warrior (1 Sam. 8:19–20; 2 Sam. 11:1).

In addition to the epithets of King and divine Warrior, the sovereignty of Yahweh is expressed in His actions of purposing (14:24, 27; 46:10), speaking (9:8; 31:2; 40:8; 45:23; 55:10–11), and exercising power for both judgment and blessing (1:25; 9:11; 10:4; 40:2; 41:20; 43:13; 51:5, 9; 52:10; 59:16; 60:21; see also the potter-clay motif in 29:16; 45:9; 64:8). The incomparability of Yahweh in such areas as creation (45:5–7, 18; 48:13) and predictive prophecy (41:4; 43:9; 44:6–8; 45:20–22; 46:9–10) supports His unique sovereignty and kingship. Likewise, His holiness is connected to His kingship in Isaiah 6:1–5, where Isaiah is also commissioned as Yahweh's royal messenger.[59] The epithet "the Holy One of Israel" is distributed evenly throughout Isaiah in both the judgment portions (e.g., 1:4; 5:16–24; 30:11; 31:1; 37:23; 47:4) and the restoration portions (e.g., 10:20; 12:6; 17:7; 29:19; 30:15; 40:25; 41:14, 16, 20; 43:3, 14–15; 45:11; 48:17; 49:7; 54:5; 55:5; 60:9, 14). Yahweh is further characterized by righteousness, one of the attributes of the ideal ruler in the Old Testament (e.g., 45:21).

Thus it is seen that, as Israel's King, Yahweh establishes His sovereignty in judgment that leads to the restoration of the divine ideal. Israel's King is not only Judge, He is also Deliverer-Restorer (33:22).

---

58. "Preface" to *The Holy Bible: New International Version* (Grand Rapids: Zondervan, 1978), p. ix.

59. Cf. John S. Holladay, Jr., "Assyrian Statecraft and the Prophets of Israel," *Harvard Theological Review* 63 (January 1970):30–33.

Yahweh's kingdom on earth, with its righteous Ruler and his righteous subjects, is the goal toward which the book of Isaiah steadily moves. The divine ideal for the earth will be realized. The restored earth will hear the praises of a restored people as they sing the praises of their King. To Isaiah, then, the restored earth and the restored people will conform to the divine ideal, and all will redound to the praise and glory of the Holy One of Israel for what *he* has accomplished.[60]

Isaiah's eschatology. Isaiah's view of "things to come" demonstrates his view of the incomparable, holy God who through judgment and deliverance/restoration establishes His sovereign rule through all the earth, and over Israel in particular. Thus Yahweh's sovereignty is demonstrated not only in creation but also by His control of history, in which He moves toward the goal of establishing His kingdom by judging and restoring all things.

However, Isaiah had a limited perspective from which to view the chronological fulfillment of the great events that Yahweh announced through him. The following chart illustrates how Isaiah observed the divinely revealed mountain peaks of future events without perceiving the intervening valleys of history between them. From his perspective at the end of the eighth century B.C., Isaiah's perception merged near-at-hand and far-off events into one picture.

1. Yahweh's sovereignty is established through judgment. But the judgment emphasized in chapters 1–39 leads to the ultimate restoration of the divine ideal. Israel's divine election not only provided priority in blessing, it also demanded priority in judgment. Thus Israel is the most-frequently mentioned object of Yahweh's judgment in Isaiah (cf. Isa. 5:1–7). The immediate cause for Israel's judgment was the nation's miserable response to Yahweh's demand for faith in Himself and obedience to the Torah, which would have resulted in moral purity and social justice (1:16–17; 33:14–16; 40:3–4; 56:1; 58:6–7). Thus Israel

---

60. Kenneth L. Barker, "Toward a Theology of Isaiah" (class notes, Dallas Theological Seminary, 1978), p. 11. The preceding survey of Isaiah's doctrine of God has been condensed primarily from this source.

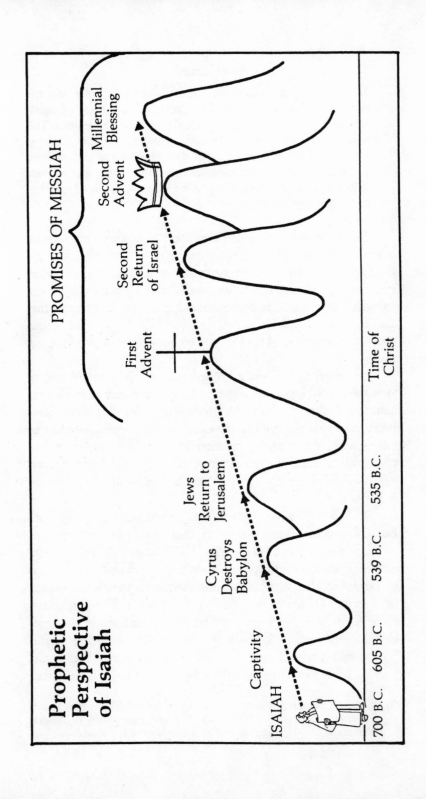

Prophetic Perspective of Isaiah

PROMISES OF MESSIAH

ISAIAH

Captivity

Cyrus Destroys Babylon

Jews Return to Jerusalem

First Advent

Second Return of Israel

Second Advent

Millennial Blessing

| 700 B.C. | 605 B.C. | 539 B.C. | 535 B.C. | Time of Christ |

was guilty of breach of Yahweh's covenant. Israelites expressed unbelief by relying on themselves (22:11; 30:12), foreign powers (8:6–8; 30:1–5; 31:1–3), ritualism (1:10–15; 58:2–7; 66:1–3), and idolatry (2:8, 20; 57:5, 13; 65:3, 7). That resulted in social injustice (5:7; 10:2; 59:8, 14–15) and immorality (1:10; 5:11–12).[61]

The ultimate purpose of Yahweh's judgment on Israel was to purify and restore the nation, producing righteousness and justice (1:26; 4:4; 32:15–20; 40:2), purging idolatry (30:22; 31:7), and producing faith (10:20). All this was to glorify Himself (2:11, 17).

Yahweh will also "punish the world for its evil" (13:11). That includes the individual nations of Assyria (10:5–19; 37:22–38), Babylon (13:19; 47:1–15), Moab (15:1—16:14; 25:10–12), Tyre (23:1–9), and Egypt (19:1–25). Major reasons for Yahweh's judgment on the Gentile nations are their arrogant rebellion against God (13:11) and their oppression of His covenant people, Israel. Again Yahweh's ultimate purpose in this judgment is to glorify Himself (33:10; 45:6; 66:18–19).

The source of judgment is Yahweh Himself (63:1–6), but He uses various instruments of judgment: Assyria and Babylon to judge Israel; Cyrus (41:25; 45:1–13) and ultimately the Davidic Messiah (11:4) along with Israel (cf. 11:14; 19:17; 41:14–16) to judge the nations. Yahweh also judges through the supernatural means of His Word (9:8; 14:26–27; 17:13; 24:3; 66:15) and His sword (a metaphor for supernatural judgment, 31:8; 34:5–6; 66:16). He also uses natural means such as earthquakes (13:13; 29:6) and hailstones (30:30).

A principle of progressive fulfillment is present in the chronology of judgment. Some of Isaiah's announcements of judgment were fulfilled in the Assyrian and Babylonian captivities. Others await a future end-time fulfillment (13:9–13; 34:8–10). The ultimate judgment of the wicked is eternal in character

61. Much of the reference information for this section is taken from Jack S. Deere, "A Theology of Isaiah" (student paper for Old Testament Theology III, Dallas Theological Seminary, Fall 1978).

(66:24). Isaiah's perspective sometimes merges those events (see illustration above).

2. Yahweh's sovereignty is established in deliverance/restoration. Isaiah 40–66 places emphasis on the restoration of all things to the divine ideal. However, the restoration theme is limited to a remnant because, although the purpose of the judgment is restorative, its punitive features involve eternal judgment on the wicked. Thus a recurring theme in Isaiah is Yahweh's preservation and restoration of a "remnant" of Israel. Some of those passages refer to a non-eschatological remnant that survives the Assyrian and Babylonian invasions (1:4–9; 6:9–13; 7:2–9; 30:15–17). However, a significant group of passages relates to the eschatological remnant of Israel that survives Yahweh's end-time judgments, is morally purified by Him, and enters into the blessings of the messianic kingdom (4:2–6; 10:20–23; 11:11–16; 65:8–10; cf. Rom. 11:26).

The remnant in Isaiah 24:13–16 seems to be a group of redeemed Gentiles. Gentiles in the restored kingdom will be saved on an equal basis with Israel (19:23–25; 42:1, 4, 6; 49:6; 56:1–8) but will also function in a political role subservient to Israel (45:14, 22–25; 55:5; 61:5).

The agents or instruments used by Yahweh to accomplish salvation and restoration are expounded by Isaiah in the twin themes of the Davidic Messiah and the Servant of Yahweh, and in the concepts of the Word (45:22–25; 55:10–13) and the Spirit of Yahweh (32:15; 34:16; 44:3; 59:21). Israel (55:4–5) and Cyrus (41:25–29; 44:28—45:7) also function in restorative roles.

Although Yahweh uses various agents to accomplish deliverance, He Himself is Israel's Redeemer and Family Protector (גֹּאֵל, gō'ēl). As circumstances warranted, it was the obligation of the gō'ēl toward a family member to buy back lost property (Lev. 25:25), to secure freedom (Lev. 25:47–53), to avenge the life of a murdered relative (Num. 35:16–29; Deut. 19:6, 12), or to raise posterity for the deceased (Ruth 4:5, 10; Deut. 25:5–10). Yahweh performs all those functions for Israel. As gō'ēl He is Israel's Father (Isa. 63:16; 64:7) and Husband (54:5), who redeems their property by regathering them to the land (54:1–8), their freedom by delivering them from captivity (43:1-4; 48:20; 52:11-12) and avenging their tormentors (47:4-11; 49:25-26; 64:4), and their future by securing their posterity (61:8-9).

The certainty of the deliverance/restoration is based on Yahweh's faithfulness in fulfilling the Abrahamic, Davidic, and New Covenants. The ultimate character of the restored earth involves a return to paradisiacal conditions with the Edenic curse removed (51:3), nature transformed (29:17; 41:17-20; 51:3; 55:13), animals tamed (11:6-8; 35:9; 43:20; 65:25), and universal peace and justice prevalent (2:4; 9:3; 19:23-25; 25:4; 29:19-21).

Israel will be delivered from her enemies and return to the land (26:15; 27:12-13; 41:14-16; 48:20-21; 51:10-11; 52:12; 60:21). Israel will enjoy an exalted position of world sovereignty and material prosperity (45:14; 49:22-23; 54:4, 15-17; 58:11; 60:10-14; 61:5-9), and Jerusalem will be restored and exalted (2:2-3; 44:26-28; 49:14-18; 52:1-10; 60:1-22; 66:10-13). Israel will experience forgiveness of sins (27:9; 40:2; 43:25; 44:22) and will be righteous in character (60:21) because of the work of the Spirit (32:15-17; 44:3; 59:21) and the Messiah (9:6; 16:5; 32:1; 42:1-4; 53:4-12). The nations will look to Israel for a knowledge of God (55:5; 60:3), acknowledge God's sovereignty (45:6, 23; 49:26), and worship Him (56:6-8; 66:23). The glorious messianic kingdom will extend beyond its millennial phase into all eternity (9:6; 34:17; 35:10; 45:17; 51:6, 8, 11; 59:21; 60:15, 21; 61:8). Yahweh will create a new heaven and new earth (65:17; 66:22), thus consummating the restoration of His created order. All of Yahweh's saving activity is to bring glory to Himself (26:15; 41:20; 43:7, 25; 48:9, 11; 52:5-6; 60:21; 61:3).

3. Isaiah's prophecies include unfulfilled themes. Many of Isaiah's prophecies have already been fulfilled in the Assyrian and Babylonian captivities, in Israel's return from Exile, and especially in the birth, life, sufferings, death, resurrection, and exaltation of Christ at His first advent. However, many more of Isaiah's prophetic themes await future fulfillment in connection with Christ's second advent, millennial reign, and the eternal state. Merrill F. Unger has listed eight of those unfulfilled themes:

(1) A period of apocalyptic judgment called "the Day of the LORD" will come on apostate Israel and wicked Gentiles to make way for the messianic kingdom (2:10-22; 4:1; 13:9-13; 24:1-23; 32:1-20; 63:1-6).

(2) The Jewish remnant will be purged out of the tribulation period for millennial blessing (12:1-6; 25:1-12; 26:1-19; 33:24; 35:10; 43:25; 44:22; 46:13; 54:6-10; 61:6; 62:12; 66:8).

(3) Israel will be restored to Palestine for the millennial kingdom (11:10-12; 14:1-2; 27:12-13; 35:10; 43:5-6; 49:10-12; 66:20).

(4) Israel will be exalted as head of the nations in the Millennium (2:1-5; 4:2-6; 11:4-16; 14:1-3; 25:1-12; 32:15-20; 35:1-10; 52:1-12; 59:20-21; 60:1-12; 61:3—62:12; 65:17—66:24).

(5) The land of Palestine will be restored (30:23-26; 35:1-10; 49:19; 60:13; 61:4; 62:4-5; 65:21-25).

(6) Jerusalem will be the capital of the millennial earth (1:26; 2:3; 4:2-6; 12:6; 24:23; 26:1; 40:2; 52:1-12; 60:1-22; 62:1-7).

(7) Blessing will rest on the nations in the Millennium (2:1-4; 11:3-4, 9-10; 25:6-9; 60:1-12).

(8) Blessing will extend to all of creation in the new heavens and new earth in the eternal state (65:17; 66:22).[62]

Isaiah's doctrine of the Messiah. Yahweh as King has determined to administer His theocratic rule through instruments chosen to represent Him and effect His will and righteous order on all the earth. Those human mediatorial rulers (kings) were to be a reflection of the kingship of Yahweh and were typical of the ideal messianic King to come.

The concept of the Davidic king as "Yahweh's anointed" describes the intimate relationship between Yahweh and the king whom He has chosen as His servant (2 Sam. 3:18; 7:5), adopted as His son (1 Chron. 22:10; 28:6), and endowed with His Spirit (1 Sam. 16:13). That relationship was based on the inviolable

62. Merrill F. Unger, *Unger's Commentary on the Old Testament* (Chicago: Moody, 1981), 2:1133-34.

covenant that Yahweh made with David and His royal line to fulfill this mediatorial role, which would ultimately culminate in the Messiah.[63]

The provisions of the Davidic covenant included personal promises to David (2 Sam. 7:8–11a) but centered on the dynastic promise of 2 Samuel 7:11b: "The LORD declares to you that the LORD himself will establish a house for you." That promise to David, to be fulfilled in his posterity, was then expanded along four lines: (1) the promise of an eternal seed (vv. 12, 16); (2) the promise of an eternal kingdom, or realm (v. 16); (3) the promise of an eternal throne, or exercise of rulership (vv. 13, 16); and (4) the establishment of a Father-son relationship between Yahweh and the king (v. 14). Such a Father-son relationship involves the aspect of chastening, but that in no way modifies the unilateral nature of the covenant, nor makes it conditional on human obedience for its ultimate fulfillment (vv. 14–15). The ultimate fulfillment of the Son of David is messianic, for an eternal dynasty, an eternal kingdom, and an eternal throne (2 Sam. 7:16) are impossible unless the line of descendants culminates in an eternal person. That Jesus Christ would be that descendant of David who would rule on the throne of David over the kingdom of Israel forever was clearly announced to Mary by angelic testimony (Luke 1:31–33). Thus the Davidic covenant added concreteness to the messianic idea by establishing that (1) the promised Deliverer would be the anointed King, establishing

63. The word messiah is derived from the Hebrew מָשִׁיחַ (māshîaḥ, "anointed"). This Hebrew word is transliterated into Greek as μεσσίας (messias), which is then transliterated as "Messias" in the King James Version (in the New Testament only in John 1:41; 4:25). The Hebrew word is translated "Messiah" only twice in the Old Testament (KJV, Dan. 9:25–26). In its other Old Testament occurrences (thirty-seven other times) the King James Version translates it "anointed" (four times of the high priest, Lev. 4:3, 5, 16; 6:22; twice of the patriarchs, Ps. 105:15; 1 Chron. 16:22; and the remaining times of the king, usually of Israel, but even Cyrus the Persian whom Yahweh elevated as king and chose as His instrument, Isa. 45:1). The thirty-nine instances of māshîaḥ in the Old Testament are all translated in the LXX by the Greek χριστός (christos, "anointed"), which is the frequent title (and later proper name) applied to Jesus in the New Testament (transliterated in most English versions as "Christ").

divine sovereignty on the earth, and (2) the King would be the Son of David.

Thus in the narrower sense the Old Testament concept of Messiah denoted the ideal Davidic king in whom would be fulfilled all the promises of the Davidic covenant (2 Sam. 7:5-16). So by New Testament times the expression "Son of David" was a synonym for the "Messiah" (Matt. 21:9; Mark 10:47-48).

However, in a broader sense, the messianic concept embraces all Old Testament prophecies of a coming mediatorial Deliverer. In that sense the Messiah included such prophetic figures as the Prophet like Moses (Deut. 18:15-19; cf. Acts 3:22-23; 7:37; John 5:45-47), the Branch (Jer. 23:5; 33:15; Zech. 3:8; 6:12), the Son of man (Dan. 7:13-14), and the coming of Yahweh Himself as Deliverer (Joel 3:16-17; Amos 1:2; Hos. 3:5; Ezek. 34:11-12; Mal. 3:1). Isaiah's Servant of Yahweh should be included in that list because, as will be seen in the commentary below, the Servant is a royal figure chosen as Yahweh's Servant and endowed with His Spirit (Isa. 42:1-2).

The prophecy of Isaiah is, in many respects, the high-water mark of messianic prophecy. The great trilogy of messianic prophecies in chapters 7, 9, and 11 pictures in rich colors the image of King Messiah, who had previously been seen only in shadowy outline. Although there are numerous views as to the contemporary significance of Isaiah's Immanuel prophecy (7:14),[64] Matthew clearly saw it as fulfilled in the virgin birth of Jesus Christ (Matt. 1:18-25).

The prophecy in Isaiah 9:1-7 indicates that the nation Israel (represented by Galilee) will be the recipient of spiritual light that will lead to rejoicing (vv. 1-3). The rejoicing is grounded in three facts: (1) the cessation of oppression (v. 4), (2) the destruction of the weapons of war (v. 5), and (3) the presence of the Prince of Peace (vv. 6-7). In verse 6, the birth of the child clearly alludes to Messiah's descent from David (and of course, then, His human nature). Although some have interpreted the gift of "a son" as implying Messiah's deity, the apparent synonymous

---

64. See Edward E. Hindson, *Isaiah's Immanuel: A Sign of His Times or the Sign of the Ages?* (Grand Rapids: Baker, 1979).

parallelism between "a child is born" and "a son is given" identifies the latter phrase as another reference to His Davidic descent. The reference to government in verses 6 and 7 identifies His Davidic kingship, and the fourfold throne name denotes His deity: "And he will be called Wonderful Counselor, Mighty God, Everlasting Father, Prince of Peace" (v. 6b). Those divine characteristics of Messiah will receive their fullest expression when He sits on the throne of David and rules over David's kingdom (v. 7).

Just as David the son of Jesse sprang from an insignificant family in Bethlehem, even so, at such a time as the royal line of David has been reduced to a similar obscurity, in an insignificant family in Bethlehem the Messiah will spring forth. So a descendant of David will sprout again when "a shoot will come up from the stump of Jesse; from his roots a Branch will bear fruit" (Isa. 11:1). The messianic Branch will bear fruit because of the anointing of the Holy Spirit (v. 2), and He will conduct a righteous rule (vv. 3–5) in a kingdom of peace (vv. 6–9).

The messianic identification of the suffering Servant has been noted above and will be defended in the commentary to follow. However, because Isaiah 61:1–3 has not been included as a Servant song in this book, that great messianic passage deserves comment. The passage has close affinity with the Servant Songs. The ministries of the one speaking are similar to those previously attributed to the Servant. Jesus inaugurated His teaching ministry in Nazareth by quoting it and then affirming, "Today this scripture is fulfilled in your hearing" (Luke 4:21). It is significant that He "rolled up the scroll" (v. 20) after stopping His reading in the middle of a sentence with the words "to proclaim the year of the Lord's favor" (Luke 4:19). He did that because the next event referred to—"the day of vengeance of our God" (Isa. 61:2)—is not to be fulfilled until His second advent (cf. Isa. 34:8; 35:4–10; 2 Thess. 1:7–10).

The categories of messianic prophecy need to be discussed to aid in clarifying the identity of the figure in Isaiah's Servant Songs. Franz J. Delitzsch distinguishes five classes, or categories, in his discussion of messianic psalms.[65] Because the categories

65. Franz J. Delitzsch, *Biblical Commentary on the Psalms*, 1871 ed., 1:68–71.

apply to all messianic prophecy, they will be mentioned with brief explanations and illustrations.

The simplest form is the *purely prophetic* passage, which is thus directly messianic. In this type of prophecy the person described and the actions indicated refer only to the Lord Jesus Christ without any kind of immediate reference to any other son of David or other Old Testament figure. Psalm 110, which is quoted more often in the New Testament than any other psalm, was cited by Christ as referring directly to Himself as Messiah (Matt. 22:41–45; Mark 12:35–37; Luke 20:44; 22:69; cf. Acts 2:34–35; 1 Cor. 15:25; Heb. 1:13; 10:13). Although Psalm 110 is probably the only purely prophetic psalm,[66] there are many other such prophecies in the Old Testament (e.g., Dan. 7:13–14; Zech. 9:9–10). It is my position that all four of the Servant Songs (Isa. 42:1–9; 49:1–13; 50:4–11; 52:13—53:12) belong in this category.[67]

In contrast to the first category are *typically messianic* prophecies. A number of such passages occur where the psalmist speaks of himself and his own experience, and in certain features he is a type or "picture prophecy" of Christ (e.g., Ps. 69:4, 21, 25; cf. John 15:25; 19:28–30; Acts 1:16–20; see also Ps. 41:9; cf. John 13:18). Robert Culver states, "By Typical Messianic Prophecy of Scripture is meant description of events, institutions and persons such as certain prophets [e.g., Moses in Deut. 18:14–22], priests [cf. Zech. 6:9–15; Heb. 2–7] and kings (especially) of the Davidic dynasty, designed by God to be distinctly prophetic of Messiah."[68]

66. Robert D. Culver adds Psalm 2 to this category ("The Old Testament as Messianic Prophecy," *Bulletin of the Evangelical Theological Society* 7 [1964]:92). J. Barton Payne, who denies any kind of "dual fulfillment" of prophecy, adds Psalm 22 along with all other truly messianic references in the Psalms in *The Theology of the Older Testament* (Grand Rapids: Zondervan, 1962), pp. 257–84, 519–20. Cf. Payne's *Encyclopedia of Biblical Prophecy* (New York: Harper & Row, 1973), pp. 121–40.
67. Although conservative scholars generally regard Isaiah 52:13—53:12 as "directly messianic," there is less agreement regarding the category to which the other three Servant Songs belong.
68. Culver, "Messianic Prophecy," p. 93. Kenneth L. Barker, in an unpublished outline, includes in this category the royal psalms, in which historical kings are types of the ultimate Son of David, the messianic King.

The *hyperbolical-typical* or *typico-prophetically* messianic prophecies combine features of the first two categories. Thus they refer initially to the historical individual whose experience is described partly in language that is true of the historical person only in a figurative manner (i.e., by hyperbole) but finds its literal fulfillment in Jesus Christ. Thus the part of the prophecy that applies literally to the historical figure is to be fulfilled in Christ antitypically, but the part that applies to the historical person only figuratively is to be fulfilled in Christ directly. The picture of David's sufferings in Psalm 22 is a classic example of this category. Compare verse 8 with Matthew 27:43 for an illustration true of both David (literally) and Christ (antitypically, but of course literally), and verses 14 and 16 for language that goes beyond David's experience (true of him hyperbolically) but that was fulfilled in Christ directly and literally (Matt. 27:35–46; John 19:23–25).

The fourth category of prophecy is that of *indirectly messianic* passages. The basic examples of this type are many of the royal psalms (e.g., Pss. 2, 89, 72, 132), which refer to David or his royal descendant in relation to the promises of the Davidic covenant that awaited its final fulfillment in Jesus Christ, in whom the Davidic line culminates. Because the messianic hopes that centered on the historical king in those passages went unfulfilled and await fulfillment in Christ, it seems best not to refer to those psalms as typical (because the description had only an ideal and not a literal reference to any Davidic king before Christ). That is not to deny that in many passages David (individually) or the concept of Davidic kingship (collectively) may have a typical significance.

The final category introduced by Delitzsch is that of *eschatologically Yahwistic* prophecies, named after the future kingdom of Yahweh that forms their theme. Many scholars today refer to the psalms that fit into this category as "enthronement psalms" (see esp. Pss. 93; 95–99). A preferable term is "psalms of God's kingship" or "theocratic psalms." These psalms do not speak

However, a certain idealism present in many of the royal psalms would seem to make the *indirectly messianic* category (see below) more suitable.

directly of the Messiah[69] but rather of the future rule of Yahweh
on the earth, a rule that will be fulfilled mediatorially through
the Davidic Messiah-King in the Millennium. Culver subsumes
this category under one he calls "Divine Parousia Prophecies."[70]
Those prophecies connect the coming salvation with the coming
of God Himself to deal directly with the world (e.g., Isa. 40:9–
11; Mic. 1:3; Mal. 3:1; Ps. 50:3). Those passages seem appropriate as a subcategory of *eschatologically Yahwistic* prophecies, one
group dealing with Yahweh "reigning," the other with Yahweh
"coming."

69. Thus Barker, in an effort to reduce and simplify the categories, includes
    them as a subcategory under *indirectly messianic* prophecy, in which their
    literal fulfillment is by extension from God in general to the Messiah in
    particular. Barker also includes under indirectly messianic prophecy a
    subcategory called "Extension from *man* in general to the Messiah in
    particular." This is a very apt label for the unique prophecy found in
    Psalm 8 (cf. Gen. 1:26–28; Heb. 2:5–9). Barker also includes the subca-
    tegory "Extension from *concepts* in general to the Messiah in particular,"
    exemplified in the concept of "wisdom" in Proverbs 8:22–31 (cf. John
    1:1–14; 1 Cor. 1:24, 30; Col. 1:15–17; 2:3; Heb. 1:1–4; Rev. 3:14).
70. Culver, "Messianic Prophecy," p. 95. Culver also adds two more cate-
    gories. The first he calls "Messianic by Extension." Using the term
    "extension" in a somewhat different sense from Barker (see n. 69),
    Culver uses this category to refer to Christ fulfilling the ethical ideals of
    the law (e.g., Pss. 1, 5) or the practical wisdom of the Hebrew wisdom
    literature (such as the various proverbs). The very difficulty of the fulfill-
    ment of those ideals by man anticipated their fulfillment by Christ. It
    seems this category is stretching the concept of prophecy, but even more
    so in Culver's final category—"Messianic by way of Preparation"— which
    refers to God's providential workings throughout the Old Testament in
    preparing Israel for Christ's coming. Granting the truth of the concept, it
    still seems improper to refer to this preparation as a category of messianic
    prophecy.

2

The Call of the Servant:
Isaiah 42:1-9

The four Servant Songs appear in Isaiah 40-55. Those chapters contain prophecies of comfort for Israel written by Isaiah from the perspective of the Exile and the return. Isaiah 40-66 emphasizes the deliverance (40-48), the Deliverer (49-55 [or 57]), and the delivered (56 [or 58]-66). The three sections deal respectively with the purpose of peace (the comfort), the Prince of Peace (the cross), and the program of peace (the crown).

The first Servant song (42:1-9) is preceded by two major sections. In the first section Yahweh comforts His people by announcing His coming (40:1-11, a prologue), and the prophet encourages the people by demonstrating Yahweh's superiority over all possible rivals (40:12-31, a disputation). The Servant song forms the conclusion of the second section, in which Yahweh proves He controls history by demonstrating His ability to prophesy (41:1—42:9). The section consists of (1) a trial speech, in which Yahweh proves His case by giving a near prophecy of His choice of Cyrus as a righteous liberator (41:1-7); (2) two salvation oracles and a proclamation of salvation, in which Yahweh gives a distant prophecy of Israel's final triumph over her

foes (41:8–20); and (3) another trial speech, in which Yahweh
reaffirms His control of history and prophecy (41:21—42:9).[1] In
the final unit (41:21—42:9) Yahweh challenges the idols to present their case (41:21-24) and responds with two prophecies: a
near prophecy of the victories of Cyrus (41:25-29) and a distant
prophecy of His Servant who will bring salvation and order to
the earth (42:1-9).

In the first Servant song[2] Yahweh gives a distant, or long-
range, prophecy of His Servant[3] who will bring salvation and
establish a proper order on the whole earth. The emphasis of the

1. For a discussion of the various forms of literary genre in prophetic litera-
   ture, see Claus Westermann, *Basic Forms of Prophetic Speech* (Philadelphia:
   Westminster, 1967); cf. Westermann, "The Way of Promise Through the
   Old Testament," in *The Old Testament and Christian Faith*, ed.
   Bernhard W. Anderson (New York: Harper & Row, 1963), pp. 200-20.
   See also Antoon Schoors, *I Am God Your Saviour: A Form Critical Study of
   the Main Genres in Is. XL—LV* (Leiden: E. J. Brill, 1973); Roy F. Melugin,
   The Formation of Isaiah 40-55 (New York: Walter de Gruyter, 1976);
   Robert B. Chisolm, "Toward a Form Critical/Structural Analysis of Isaiah" (student paper, Dallas Theological Seminary, 1980).
2. Isaiah 42:1-9 is usually viewed as three paragraphs (vv. 1-4, vv. 5-7, and
   vv. 8-9), but the extent of the "Servant song" is disputed. Verses 1-4
   constitute the basic unit, but how much further (if any) does the reference
   to the Servant extend? Liberal critical scholars of a former generation not
   only viewed the basic unit (vv. 1-4) as an addition to the text of Deutero-
   Isaiah but also regarded verses 5-9 as still later accretions (e.g., Bernhard
   Duhm, 1892). However, more recent scholarship accepts both the (Deu-
   tero-) Isaianic authorship of 42:1-4 and, for the most part, the unity of
   that passage with its following context. Thus a number of scholars include
   42:1-7 in the first Servant song (e.g., Sigmund Mowinckel, 1921), whereas
   others extend it through verse 9, as I do. Some think 42:5-9 is a separate
   Servant song: see Christopher R. North, *The Suffering Servant in Deutero-
   Isaiah: An Historical and Critical Study*, 2d ed. (London: Oxford U., 1956),
   pp. 131-32; H. H. Rowley, *The Servant of the Lord and Other Essays on the
   Old Testament* (Oxford: Basil Blackwell, 1952), p. 6, n. 1.
3. The identification of the Servant in this poem generally coincides with the
   interpreter's overall view of the identity of the Servant throughout the
   Servant Songs. Cundall, however, views verses 1-4 as speaking of the
   Messiah but verses 5-9 as speaking of Cyrus (Arthur E. Cundall, *Isaiah
   40-66 and Jeremiah*, Scripture Union Bible Study Books [Grand Rapids:
   Eerdmans, 1969], p. 6) However, Cyrus was never "a covenant for the
   people," nor did he bring "light" (i.e., salvation) to the Gentiles (v. 6).
   The parallels with 49:8 indicate verses 5-7 are referring to the Servant-
   Messiah.

passage is on the introduction of the Servant and the outcome of His completed task. The Servant is called to accomplish His work. The poem thus announces the Servant's faithfulness in fulfilling the mission for which He was designated.

Yahweh is the Speaker throughout the poem.[4] Verses 1–4 are apparently addressed to all mankind (certainly to all who hear of this designation of Yahweh's Servant[5]) and constitute Yahweh's designatory call of and promised accomplishments by His Servant. Verses 5–7 are spoken directly to the Servant as a promise of the divine empowerment needed for the accomplishment of His task. Verses 8–9 are God's self-predication based on fulfilled prophecy and addressed to His people Israel in exile. The first Servant poem thus includes these points: (1) Yahweh predicts His Servant's success in causing a just order to prevail in the earth (vv. 1–4), (2) Yahweh promises to empower His Servant in the accomplishment of His righteous rule (vv. 5–7), and (3) Yahweh directs glory to Himself by the use of prophecy (vv. 8–9).

YAHWEH PREDICTS SUCCESS
FOR HIS SERVANT (42:1–4)

[1]Here is my servant, whom I uphold,
   my chosen one in whom I delight;
I will put my Spirit on him
   and he will bring justice to the nations.
[2]He will not shout or cry out,
   or raise his voice in the streets.
[3]A bruised reed he will not break,
   and a smoldering wick he will not snuff out.
In faithfulness he will bring forth justice;

4. Isaiah 42:5 conveys the typical "messenger formula," introductory to the words of Yahweh in verses 6–7.
5. The view of R. N. Whybray that these verses are addressed to Yahweh's "heavenly council" lacks support in the passage (*Isaiah 40–66* [Grand Rapids: Eerdmans, 1981], p. 71).

⁴ he will not falter or be discouraged
till he establishes justice on earth.
In his law the islands will put their hope.

W. A. M. Beuken has demonstrated that the literary genre of
this strophe is very similar to Yahweh's designations of kings (see
the divine designations of Saul [1 Sam. 9:17], David [1 Sam.
16:12–13], and even Zerubbabel [Zech. 3:8; 6:12]). The strophe
has the following features in common with acts by which Yahweh
designates His king: (1) the designation is by Yahweh and is
mostly expressed with "behold"; (2) Yahweh endows the chosen
one with His Spirit; and (3) mishpāt (a just order) is the characteristic task of the royal figure.⁶

In this strophe Yahweh (1) designates His Servant, who will
establish a just order through His Spirit (v. 1); (2) describes the
service of His Servant, who will neither seek publicity nor promote violence (vv. 2–3a); (3) describes the success of the Servant's mission (v. 3b); and (4) declares the unfailing endurance
of His Servant (v. 4).

YAHWEH DESIGNATES AND ENDOWS HIS SERVANT (42:1)

Yahweh identifies His Servant to others and with Himself
(v. 1a). Before Yahweh affirms His Servant's endowment with His
Spirit and His Servant's resultant success, Yahweh first identifies
His Servant *to* others and *with* Himself: "Here is⁷ my servant
whom I uphold, my chosen one in whom I delight." This introduction of the Servant by Yahweh to all who will hear is pro-

6. W. A. M. Beuken "Mišpāṭ: The First Servant Song and Its Context," *Vetus
Testamentum* 22 (1972):3. Cf. John H. Eaton, *Festal Drama in Deutero-
Isaiah* (London: S.P.C.K., 1979), pp. 47–48. Westermann has mentioned
a feature that further distinguishes this designation from a prophetic call
narrative (as in Isa. 6): The prophet's call never has human witnesses,
whereas the king's call requires such witnesses (Claus Westermann, *Isaiah
40–66: A Commentary* [Philadelphia: Westminster, 1975], p. 94). However, not all scholars who identify this unit as a designation oracle limit it
to the designation of a royal personage (e.g., Melugin, *Formation of Isaiah*,
pp. 66–67).
7. The opening *hēn* ("Behold," KJV; "Here is," NIV) contrasts with the *hēn*
of 41:29, which introduces the impotent idols chosen by the nations.
Yahweh's Servant is divinely powerful.

phetic of the Servant's appointment and call to office as the Messiah.[8]

The fresh introduction of the Servant, after reference had already been made to Israel as "servant" in 41:8–9, suggests that this Servant differs from Israel. It is generally recognized, at least by evangelicals, that this Servant song is speaking of an individual rather than Israel personified, even though, for example, 42:1-7 and 49:1-13 have a number of characteristics in common (see n. 7, chap. 3). This Servant accomplishes the task for which the nation was responsible but unqualified (42:18-22)—the task of bringing light to the Gentiles and establishing a just worldwide order. Allan A. MacRae notes that the "marked contrast" between 42:1-7 and 42:18-22 "would be very difficult to explain, apart from the recognition that the latter deals with the responsibility of the nation as a whole, while the former is concerned with the actual accomplishment of the task."[9] In the Servant Songs as a whole there is a contrast between the individual Servant and the national servant Israel. The servant Israel has to be admonished to trust God (40:27-31; 41:8-10, 14-16; 42:18-19), is sinful and has been punished for her sins (40:1-2; 42:22-25; 43:22-28; 47:6; 50:1; 54:4-8), complains bitterly (40:27; 49:14; 50:1-2), and is the recipient, not the agent, of salvation. On the other hand, the individual Servant expresses total trust in God (50:7-9), is innocent and suffers for the sins of others (50:5-6; 53:4-6, 9, 11-12), suffers patiently (53:7), and performs a ministry on behalf of the nations and Israel (49:5-6).

Yahweh willingly acknowledges the Servant as "my servant," thus indicating that the Servant belongs to and has a close relationship with Yahweh Himself. In fact "my servant" is an expression parallel to "my chosen one," suggesting that the divine choice or election is the foundation for the honorable position of and faithful performance by the Servant. Election by Yahweh made a person His Servant (cf. 1 Kings 11:13, 32-34; Ps.

8. The words of the Father at the baptism of Jesus combine this passage with Psalm 2:7, suggesting the identity of the Isaianic Servant with the Davidic Messiah.
9. Allan A. MacRae, "The Servant of the Lord in Isaiah," *Bibliotheca Sacra* 121 (April–June 1964): 132.

105:26; Hag. 2:23). The Servant's task cannot be performed by just anyone; it can be accomplished only by Yahweh's "chosen one." Election and service go hand in hand (43:10–12, 21; cf. 41:8–9). The expression "my servant" is not only a title of honor,[10] but also, because Yahweh is viewed as the King of Israel in the immediate context (41:21; cf. 43:15; 44:6), a description implying royal associations.

Recognition of the Servant as a royal figure in this passage contributes to the identification of the Servant with the Davidic Messiah. Although it is true that terms such as "my servant" and "my chosen one" are not exclusively royal terms, there is evidence that the passage views the Servant primarily as a royal personage. For example, not only is the literary genre of the passage similar to a royal designation oracle (as already indicated), but the task of establishing מִשְׁפָּט (mishpāṭ, "a just order") is a characteristically royal responsibility. Dirk H. Odendaal has demonstrated that the Servant is a royal personage and that "the identification of the Suffering Servant and the Messiah did not take place for the first time in the self-consciousness of Jesus, but it was there from the beginning." However, Odendaal also recognizes that the terminology describing the Servant is not completely royal, for in the Servant "the priestly and prophetic offices find their divinely ordained integration in and subordination to the royal office."[11]

As indicated by David F. Payne, "the language seems to link kingly and prophetic characteristics in a role reminiscent of that of Moses. It is as if to say that the Second Exodus, such a major theme in these chapters [Isa. 40–55], will require a Second Moses."[12] That is a helpful identification when one recognizes the

---

10. See chapter 1 for the meaning of the word 'ebed ("servant").
11. Dirk H. Odendaal, The Eschatological Expectation of Isaiah 40–66 with Special Reference to Israel and the Nations (Nutley, N.J.: Presbyterian and Reformed, 1970), pp. 129–35.
12. David F. Payne, "Isaiah," in The New Layman's Bible Commentary, ed. G. C. D. Howley, F. F. Bruce, and H. L. Ellison (Grand Rapids: Zondervan, 1979), p. 800. Westermann, Isaiah 40–66 (p. 97), suggests that the functions of prophet (mediator by word of mouth) and king (mediator by action), which parted company after Moses' time, are reunited in the Servant.

royal function of Moses as vice-regent under Yahweh at the establishment of the Sinaitic covenant.[13] The royal features of the Servant forge a link between the concepts of the royal Davidic Messiah and the suffering Servant.[14] Thus it may be concluded with Odendaal that the Servant is "a royal, individual, eschatological figure, who is instrumental in bringing about the royal eschatological dominion of Yahweh."[15]

To resume the exposition, the identification of the Servant with Yahweh is indicated not only in the titles designating the Servant ("my servant" and "my chosen one") but also in the phrases describing their relationship ("whom I uphold" [i.e., grasp by the hand, e.g., Ex. 17:12; Prov. 31:19] and "in whom I delight"). Yahweh sustains His Servant by upholding Him with strength as God the Creator (cf. v. 5; see also Yahweh's help for the Servant in 42:6; 49:8; 50:7). The entire expression, "my servant, whom I uphold," is tantamount to saying, "He is mine— no power can overcome Him!"[16] How can He not succeed in His task of causing a just order to prevail in the earth?

Yahweh speaks of His selected Servant as one "in whom I delight." Although in the Hebrew perfect tense, the verb "delight" probably refers to Yahweh's habitual delight in the Servant and is not to be limited to the moment of choice.[17] In summary,

13. Under the leadership of Moses, God formed Israel into a nation on the basis of election and redemption, and He established Himself as her King (Ex. 19–24; 32–34; cf. Deut.; Josh. 24). The kingship of Yahweh is a prominent concept in the history of Israel (See chap. 1, notes 52 and 53 for references and bibliography). Moses, the covenant mediator, his successor Joshua, and later the judges functioned much like kings during the premonarchial period of the theocracy. Then with the beginning of the monarchial period, the kings functioned as vice-regents under Yahweh, who was still King of Israel.

14. The sufferings of the Servant, barely hinted at in this first poem, await further expression in the other Servant songs, especially 52:13—53:12.

15. Odendaal, *Eschatological Expectation*, p. 135. Odendaal, however, does not intend this statement in a premillennial sense.

16. Cf. August Pieper, *Isaiah II: An Exposition of Isaiah 40–66* (1919; trans., Milwaukee: Northwestern, 1979), p. 178.

17. The alternation between the imperfect form (prefix conjugation) and the perfect form (suffix conjugation) expresses Yahweh's habitual support of and delight in the Servant.

then, Yahweh sustains His Servant whom He has specified and
savors His Servant whom He has selected.

   *Yahweh declares that He will endow His Servant with the power
of the Spirit (v. 1b).* The prediction "I will put my Spirit on him"
clarifies Yahweh's means of sustaining His Servant as indicated in
the preceding line: it is by the power of His own Spirit that
Yahweh assures the success of the Servant's mission. The results
of the endowment with Yahweh's Spirit are described in Isaiah
11:2-4, a messianic passage containing concepts found in the
Servant Songs. A further messianic passage (61:1-3; cf. Luke
4:17-21) describes the divine enablement of the Spirit for an
anointed one entrusted with a task. Such an endowment with the
Spirit of Yahweh as described in this verse is typical of the special
gift of the Spirit often given to empower the leaders of Israel.
Especially significant is the gift of Yahweh's Spirit to the Davidic
kings.[18]

   The divine endowment is conveyed in the term נָתַתִּי (*nātattî*,
"I will put"). The term is to be understood as a prophetic perfect.
It cannot be determined from this passage whether the verb refers
to a completed action of the Spirit, as with the descent like a
dove at Christ's baptism (Mark 1:11), or to Christ's continual
endowment with the Spirit for His difficult ministry (Matt.
12:28). Either nuance is possible because the Servant Messiah
obviously had a permanent (Isa. 11:2) and plenary endowment
with the Spirit, although He was particularly marked out as
Messiah by the anointing of the Spirit at the baptism that inaugurated His messianic ministry.

   *Yahweh declares that His Servant will succeed in His mission
(v. 1c).* Yahweh's declaration that He will endow His Servant
with the power of the Spirit (v. 1b) is foundational to His declaration that His Servant will succeed in His mission: "and he will
bring justice to the nations." Christopher R. North rightly calls
this statement "the key to the understanding of the passage."[19]

18. The Spirit enabled kings (1 Sam. 11:6; 16:13; cf. Isa. 11:2), prophets
    (Num. 11:29; 24:2; 2 Chron. 24:20; Ezek. 11:5; Mic. 3:8), leaders (Num.
    11:17; Judg. 3:10; 6:34) and artisans (Ex. 31:1-5).
19. Christopher R. North, *The Second Isaiah: Introduction, Translation, and
    Commentary to Chapters XL—LV* (Oxford: Clarendon, 1964), p. 107.

That is supported by the threefold reference to the Servant bringing forth or establishing justice: "He will bring justice to the nations" (v. 1c); "in faithfulness he will bring forth justice" (v. 3c); "till he establishes justice on earth" (v. 4b). The meaning of mishpāṭ, the Hebrew word translated "justice," is very significant (and is also much disputed) in this Servant song. R. N. Whybray says that it should "probably be assumed" that the word has the same meaning all three times it occurs. The validity of that assumption requires evaluation, but it is necessary first to summarize the possible meanings of mishpāṭ, which Whybray calls "a word of many meanings."[20]

The primary meaning of the noun mishpāṭ is that of a judicial decision or sentence (e.g., Num. 27:21; Deut. 16:18; 1 Kings 3:28; 20:40). A variety of derived meanings also relate in some way to the judicial process, such as the act of deciding (Deut. 25:1; Josh. 20:6), the place of decision (Deut. 25:1; 1 Kings 7:7), the process of litigation (Job 22:4; Ps. 143:2; Isa. 3:14), the case presented for litigation (1 Kings 3:11; Job 13:18; Ezek. 23:24), the time of judgment (Ps. 1:5), and the execution of the sentence (Deut. 32:41; Ezek. 18:8).[21] Also, mishpāṭ "can be used to designate almost any aspect of civil or religious government,"[22] such as sovereignty (Deut. 1:17; Jer. 8:7) or magisterial authority (Ps. 72:1–2), the attribute of justice employed by civil leaders (Mic. 3:1), an ordinance of law (Ex. 15:25; Lev. 5:10; 9:16; Deut. 33:10, 21), or one's right under law (Deut. 18:3; Jer. 32:7). The word mishpāṭ also has the meaning of that which is fitting or proper (1 Kings 5:8; Isa. 28:26; 40:14). The related verb שָׁפַט (shāpaṭ, "to judge, govern") in its primary sense means to exercise the processes of government,[23] whether legislative, executive, or judicial. God Himself is "the Judge of all the earth" (Gen. 18:25; cf. Isa. 33:22) and has delegated that function of

20. Whybray, Isaiah 40–66, p. 72.
21. Mark A. Arrington, "The Identification of the Anonymous Servant in Isaiah 40–55" (Th.M. thesis, Dallas Theological Seminary, 1971), p. 15.
22. R. Laird Harris, Gleason L. Archer, Jr., and Bruce K. Waltke, eds., Theological Wordbook of the Old Testament (Chicago: Moody, 1980), 2:948.
23. Ibid., p. 947.

judging or governing to His theocratic representatives (not to prophets) such as Moses (Ex. 18:13), the judges (e.g., Deborah [Judg. 4:5] and Samuel [1 Sam. 7:6, 15]), and the kings (1 Sam. 8:19–20; Ps. 72:1–3, 12–15).

That variety of usages raises the question of the meaning of *mishpāṭ* in Isaiah 42:1–4. Whybray is surely correct that "vague renderings" such as "revelation" or "true religion" are "hardly justified."[24] Equally unsatisfactory is Pieper's view that it refers to the gospel.[25] Because *mishpāṭ* is the key concept in the first Servant song, employed three times to emphasize the totality of the Servant's task, any translation less comprehensive than "a right order" or a similar phrase fails to take account of the far-reaching accomplishments purposed for Yahweh's Servant. The Servant's task is to rectify within history all aspects and phases of human existence—moral, religious, spiritual, political, social, economic, and so forth—in order to fulfill the prayer "Your kingdom come, your will be done on earth as it is in heaven" (Matt. 6:10).

The meaning of *mishpāṭ* in this poem depends in part on the verbs used in the three occurrences of the word. In verses 1 and 3, what is the significance of יוֹצִיא ... מִשְׁפָּט (*mishpāṭ ... yôṣi'*, "he will bring forth justice")? Does the verb mean to "proclaim" justice or to "produce" (i.e., establish) justice? The word יוֹצִיא (*yôṣi'*) has the basic meaning of "bring forth, cause to go out." North maintains that when the object of the verb is not a material object, the verb always has the meaning of "cause to go out from the mouth" or "bring forth words"—that is, "speak, impart, reveal".[26] The meaning "proclaim" is also supported by Whybray.[27] The verb has this meaning in Isaiah 48:20 (cf. 2:3). Support is claimed for that view from the citation of this verse in Matthew 12:18, where the Greek word ἀπαγγελεῖ (*apangelei*) means "he will proclaim." However, because Matthew is not

24. Whybray, *Isaiah 40–66*, p. 72. The renderings are from John L. Mc-Kenzie, *Second Isaiah*, The Anchor Bible (Garden City, N.Y.: Doubleday, 1968), p. 37; Paul Volz, cited in North, *Suffering Servant*, p. 141.
25. Pieper, *Isaiah II*, p.179.
26. North, *Second Isaiah*, p. 107.
27. Whybray, *Isaiah 40–66*, p.72.

quoting from the LXX (which has ἐξοίσει, *exoisei*), ἀπαγγελεῖ (*apangelei*, "proclaim") may be an interpretation of the Hebrew rather than a translation.

On the other hand, the verb may mean "bring forth" in the sense of "cause to appear, cause to exist, produce, establish" (as in Isa. 40:26; 54:16; 61:11; Hab. 1:4). Beuken concludes that in verses 1 and 3 *mishpāṭ* is "more a situation, a state of being, to be realized than a decision to be proclaimed . . . an event to be realized, a process and its execution resulting in relations of righteousness, the background obviously being this: that the present situation is devoid of justice."[28] Thus the conclusion of Page H. Kelley seems justified: he understands *mishpāṭ* in this passage to refer to "a just order," that is, the kind of life that will prevail on earth when all nations are brought under God's rule, to be accomplished through the instrumentality of God's Servant.[29] That is the best explanation of the meaning when understood in the sense of the Davidic kingdom of righteousness and peace that Messiah will cause to prevail on the millennial earth following His second advent. Isaiah, of course, does not distinguish between the Servant's accomplishments to be fulfilled in the first advent and those to be fulfilled in the second (cf. Isa. 61:1–3 with Luke 4:17–21).

Yahweh only summarizes the task that His Servant will accomplish: the Servant will cause a just order to prevail for the nations. The Servant's success in that mission is assured by the empowering presence of the Spirit of Yahweh, who continually rests on Him (cf. Isa. 11:2–4). Some clarification and expansion of the task of the Servant will be presented in verse 6, but the main development of the Servant's task will come only in the later songs, especially the fourth (52:13—53:12).

YAHWEH DESCRIBES THE CHARACTER OF HIS SERVANT'S SERVICE (42:2–3a)

Yahweh's affirmation of His Servant's success (v. 3b) is preceded by a description of the Servant's service (vv. 2–3a). This

28. Beuken, "Mišpāṭ," p. 7.
29. Page H. Kelley, *Judgment and Redemption in Isaiah* (Nashville: Broadman, 1968), p. 63. Kelley, however, does not seem to identify this just order with the millennial Davidic kingdom from the premillennial viewpoint.

description includes five negative verbs (followed by two more in
v. 4). The most probable interpretation of the verbs indicates
that the Servant will be humble (He will not seek publicity, v. 2),
and He will be gentle toward the oppressed (v. 3a). An alternate
view, that the Servant will not utter lamentation in His distress,
is a definite possibility and merits some attention.

The Servant will be meek and humble (v. 2). Yahweh indicates
that His Servant will not seek publicity, that He will not be
clamorous or ostentatious in the accomplishment of His mission:
"He will not shout or cry out, or raise his voice in the streets."
The majority of commentators interpret this verse as referring to
the nonclamorous or gentle character of the Servant's methods
in fulfilling His mission—that "He will not shout" in strife or
dispute, that "He will not quarrel or cry out" (Matt. 12:19,
citing this verse). Many of those scholars think that the negative
clauses suggest a contrast between the Servant's functions and
those of someone else, such as earlier prophets of doom or even
Yahweh's anointed one Cyrus (Isa. 45:1–13). In the latter instance, the verbs are said to describe how a worldly conqueror
performs his deeds, in contrast to the gentleness of Yahweh's
Servant. On the other hand, the statements may simply be the
figure of speech called litotes (negative, minimizing statements
used to emphasize their opposites),[30] thus indicating the meek,
humble, gentle character of the Servant (cf. Zech. 9:9; Matt.
21:5).

The alternate interpretation of this verse is that the Hebrew
verb צעק (ṣā'aq, "shout") is properly the term for crying out to
God in lamentation, a cry for relief or justice, for deliverance in
deep need or trouble (cf. Ex. 14:10; 17:4; Judg. 4:3; Ps. 107:6;
Lam. 2:18).[31] The second verb, נשא (nāśā', "cry out"), literally
means "to lift up (the voice)" as in a cry of protest (cf. Gen.
21:16; Num. 14:1; Judg. 2:4), although it can also be used of a

---

30. See Ethelbert W. Bullinger, *Figures of Speech Used in the Bible: Explained
and Illustrated* (Grand Rapids: Baker. 1968) for a detailed study of the
figures of speech referred to in this commentary.
31. Melugin asserts, "Given Deutero-Isaiah's proclivity for the language of
the psalms, *lo' yiṣ'āq* ["he will not shout"] surely means that the servant
will not utter lamentation" (*Formation of Isaiah 40–55*, p. 99).

cry of joy (Isa. 24:14; 52:8). This alternative view understands in the same way the statement "He will not . . . raise his voice in the streets," because the streets may be a place of weeping and mourning (Isa. 15:3; 24:11; 33:7). Thus the alternate interpretation is that the Servant neither laments from discouragement in oppressive conditions nor becomes defeated but rather perseveres in the task of administering justice.[32] I have chosen the first interpretation, primarily because of the New Testament usage of this passage (Matt. 12:19).

The Servant will be gentle toward the oppressed (v. 3a). The Servant's gentle approach toward the oppressed is expressed in the clauses "A bruised reed he will not break, and a smoldering wick he will not snuff out." The Servant seeks to bless, not to destroy. He is a gracious Sovereign, not a tyrant. A reed is weak to start with—and this one is cracked or partially broken (cf. 36:6). He will handle such a "bruised reed" with great care. A "smoldering wick" (lit. "flax," cf. 19:9; 43:17) is one that is almost extinguished; but He will keep it burning—not to destroy it but to enable it to perform its designated function. The "bruised reed" and the "smoldering wick" are figurative for weak and oppressed people, whether among Israel or the Gentiles, to whomever the Servant might minister.[33] Ultimately the reference

32. Arrington, "Identification of the Anonymous Servant," pp. 21–22. Kelley takes the passage to mean the Servant's sorrow will not be prolonged, that His cry of distress will be banished forever from His lips by the relief that the Lord will provide for Him (resurrection?) (Page H. Kelley, "Isaiah," in *The Broadman Bible Commentary*, ed. C. J. Allen [Nashville: Broadman, 1971], 5:307.) However, if the reference is at all to His sufferings, could it not refer to His quiet endurance of suffering where no cry for justice (for Himself) is directed toward God?

33. Melugin views the "crushed reed" and "quenched flax" as alluding to Egypt's inability to provide security—when Israel leans on the reed it breaks (Isa. 36:6; Ezek. 29:6). Thus he says that "the servant will not rely on a crushed reed and thus break it; nor will he depend upon and thus extinguish a dimly-burning wick" (*Formation of Isaiah*, p. 99). P. A. H. DeBoer identifies the "bruised reed" and "dimly-burning wick" as the Servant Himself, who will not be broken or quenched (*Second Isaiah's Message* [Leiden: E. J. Brill, 1956], pp. 9, 92–93). Walther Zimmerli suggests that the expressions come from the sphere of legal symbolism, the bruised reed referring to the death sentence, and the whole verse indicating Yahweh's establishing of justice in a surprising act of grace (Gerhard Kittel and Gerhard Friedrich, eds., *Theological Dictionary of the New Testament* [Grand Rapids: Eerdmans, 1964–76], 5:669).

is worldwide, corresponding to the extent of His messianic kingdom, in which He will cause a just order to prevail.

YAHWEH DESCRIBES THE SUCCESS OF THE SERVANT'S MISSION (42:3b)

The Servant's task to cause a just order to prevail on the earth, described in verse 1, is reaffirmed in verse 3b in the same word ("he will bring forth justice"). The full affirmation is "in faithfulness he will bring forth justice."

The word translated "in faithfulness" is לֶאֱמֶת (le'emet, "according to truth, truly"). Claus Westermann renders it "to be truth"; that is, it becomes truth, is made to prevail.[34] Perhaps the term expresses historical conformity between the reality of the fulfillment by the Servant and the prediction given by Yahweh (cf. vv. 8–9; 43:9).[35]

YAHWEH DECLARES THE UNFAILING ENDURANCE OF THE SERVANT IN ACHIEVING HIS MISSION (42:4)

The Servant will endure, and so He will ultimately succeed over any and all adversity or difficulty in establishing a right order on the earth: "He will not falter or be discouraged till he establishes justice on the earth." The unusual word selection in the Hebrew grows out of Isaiah's play on words in verses 3 and 4. The word "falter" is literally "grow dim, fade" and echoes the "smoldering" or "dimly burning" wick in verse 3. "Be discouraged" is literally "be crushed, bruised" and echoes the "bruised" reed of verse 3. The Servant will persist through a difficult situation; He will not "go to pieces" in adversity. Thus the Servant who in gentle grace does not promote violent destruction will Himself persist with unfailing endurance, will not perish under oppression in carrying out His task to completion. Franz J. Delitzsch says that "His zeal will not be extinguished, nor will anything break His strength till He shall have secured for

34. Westermann, *Isaiah 40–66*, p. 96.
35. Cf. Beuken, "Mišpāṭ," pp. 25–26.

right a firm standing on the earth."[36] This verse contains the only implication in the first Servant poem that the Servant's road to success carries Him across difficult terrain. The vale of suffering through which the Servant must pass is the subject of later poems (esp. 52:13—53:12).

The endurance of the Servant leads to the establishment of a right order—"till he establishes justice on earth." Because the verb used here with mishpāṭ is different from the verb in verses 1 and 3, and because of the parallelism between mishpāṭ ("justice") and תּוֹרָה (tôrâ, "law"), Beuken says that mishpāṭ has a different nuance in verse 4, so that it comes to mean "an ordinance, a law to be proclaimed, the juridical statute of the new situation of justice."[37] It is unlikely, however, that mishpāṭ can bear a meaning in verse 4 different from its meaning in verses 1 and 3. The repeated reference to the concept of a worldwide just order in verses 1 and 4 is stylistically an inclusio that helps to mark off verses 1–4 as the first strophe of this Servant song. The word mishpāṭ, which describes the totality of the just order that the Servant will cause to prevail on the earth, is the theological center of these verses. The use of the verb יָשִׂים (yāśîm, "to put, set, place") also supports a continuity in meaning for mishpāṭ throughout the strophe. In view of the worldwide scope of the context (the distant "islands" or "coastlands" [NASB], v. 4c) the phrase "on earth" indicates all the earth, not just Palestine.

The expectancy of the peoples for this just order is indicated: "In his law the islands will put their hope." Often tôrâ ("law, instruction") is found parallel to mishpāṭ ("justice" [Hab. 1:4; Ps. 89:31; Isa. 51:4]). It connotes "authoritative instruction for life."[38] It was given by God first through Moses but later through priests or prophets (Jer. 26:4–5). That the "islands" will put their hope in the Servant's tôrâ is understood by August

36. Franz J. Delitzsch, *Isaiah*, Commentary on the Old Testament (Grand Rapids: Eerdmans, 1973) 2:176.
37. Beuken, "*Mišpāṭ*," p. 7. Whybray sees no difference in meaning between verses 3 and 4 but understands both as "the proclamation of a prophetic message" (*Isaiah 40–66*, p. 73).
38. Lon Jay Gregg, "An Exegetical Study of Isaiah 42:1–4" (Th.M. thesis, Dallas Theological Seminary, 1979), p. 43.

Pieper as personification. But it is better to understand the figure as a metonymy for the people who inhabit the shores or islands.[39] The word translated "islands" was a vague term for distant lands along the Mediterranean coast.[40] The word translated "will put their hope" ("wait," KJV) is said by Delitzsch to mean "to wait with longing for a person's instruction" (Job 29:23).[41]

YAHWEH PROMISES EMPOWERMENT TO HIS SERVANT (42:5-7)

⁵This is what God the LORD says—
    he who created the heavens and stretched them out,
        who spread out the earth and all that comes out of it,
    who gives breath to its people,
        and life to those who walk on it:
⁶"I, the LORD, have called you in righteousness;
    I will take hold of your hand.
I will keep you and will make you
    to be a covenant for the people
    and a light for the Gentiles,
⁷to open eyes that are blind,
    to free captives from prison
    and to release from the dungeon those who sit in
    darkness."

Others have been informed of Yahweh's designation of His Servant who will cause a just order to prevail on the earth (vv. 1–4). Now Yahweh turns directly to the Servant Himself, affirms His divine call, and promises to empower Him in the accomplishment of His righteous purpose (vv. 5–7).[42] After being introduced as the sovereign Creator in order to demonstrate His incomparable ability to empower His Servant (v. 5), Yahweh affirms to the Servant His divine call (v. 6a), promises divine aid

39. Pieper, *Isaiah II*, p. 183. Bullinger (*Figures of Speech*, p. 574) identifies it as "metonymy of the subject."
40. Whybray, *Isaiah 40–66*, p. 60.
41. Delitzsch, *Isaiah* 2:177. Westermann limits the concept to an "expectancy of deliverance" (such as Israel had at the time of the Exile), not a yearning for the one true God (*Isaiah 40–66*, p. 96).
42. Melugin, *Formation of Isaiah*, p. 67.

to the Servant (v. 6b), and outlines the task in which He will help the Servant (vv. 6c–7).

YAHWEH IS ACKNOWLEDGED AS THE SOVEREIGN CREATOR (42:5)

Yahweh's creative power is evidence that He can empower the Servant to perform His mission, which is described in verses 1–4 and partially repeated and clarified in verses 6–7.[43]

Yahweh is introduced as "God the LORD" (v. 5a). Isaiah employs the standard "messenger formula" ("This is what . . . says") to introduce Yahweh as the true and only God whose sovereign power as the Creator of heaven, earth, and mankind qualifies Him to empower His Servant (cf. 40:22; 45:12) as well as to establish His claim to control history (cf. vv. 8–9). The title "God the LORD" (הָאֵל יְהוָה, *hā'ēl yhwh*) is found only here in Isaiah (cf. Ps. 85:8).

Yahweh is described as the Creator of heaven, earth, and mankind (v. 5b). The doctrine of creation is stated in "a series of participial clauses drawn from the style of the hymn of praise"[44] (cf. Isa. 40:22; Ps. 104:2–4; 136). Yahweh's creation of the atmospheric and stellar heavens is described in the clause "he who created the heavens and stretched them out," which states the literal fact of creation and then compares it in figurative language to stretching out a curtain or tent (cf. Isa. 40:22).

Yahweh's creation of the earth and its produce is next described: "who spread out the earth and all that comes out of it." This metaphor for creation comes from the activity of a goldsmith or silversmith who beats or "spreads" out the malleable metal with his tools. The creation of both the heavens and the earth is probably a merism ascribing to God the creation of all things everywhere.[45] Further, Yahweh created all mankind: "who gives breath to its people, and life to those who walk on it."

---

43. Kelley says, "The emphasis upon the creation motif is designed to awaken faith in God. One who has revealed His power in creation is surely able to redeem His people and deliver them from their enemies" (*Judgment and Redemption,* p. 63).
44. Whybray, *Isaiah 40–66,* p. 74.
45. Westermann says the passage describes "the whole range of creation by means of the two parts, heaven and earth" (*Isaiah 40–66,* p. 99).

"Breath" and "life" are here used in poetic parallelism to describe the natural life that the Creator imparts to all mankind. The word translated "people" (עַם, 'am) normally refers to a nation, particularly Israel (cf. v. 6), but here refers to mankind—"those who walk on" the earth that God has created.

YAHWEH AFFIRMS THE SERVANT'S CALL (42:6a)

Although Yahweh has been acknowledged as the sovereign Creator, before promising help to His Servant He affirms the Servant's call: "I, the LORD, have called you in righteousness." The position of "I, Yahweh" in the sentence emphasizes it: the covenant God, who has entered into a personal relationship with Israel, is the same One who has called His Servant. He is both the powerful Creator and the covenant-keeping LORD.

The affirmation of that call addressed to the Servant is comparable to the previous designation of the Servant addressed to mankind (v. 1). Both contexts emphasize the close relationship that exists between Yahweh and His Servant.

The phrase "in righteousness" (בְּצֶדֶק, b^eṣedeq), used to describe the call, is also used in 41:2 (cf. 45:13) to describe Yahweh's call of Cyrus. The language of verse 6 is also similar to the language used of Yahweh's call of the nation Israel as His servant in 41:9–10. However, the task assigned to this Servant in verses 6–7 is more far-reaching and more spiritual than any task Yahweh purposed or accomplished through Cyrus;[46] and because it is mediatorial for Israel, it could not be accomplished by Israel.

YAHWEH PROMISES THE SERVANT HELP (42:6b)

Now that the Servant is informed of His calling, He is promised divine help to fulfill the task to which He has been called: "I will take hold of your hand. I will keep you." Yahweh's action on behalf of the Servant emphasizes strengthening guid-

46. Yahweh gave Cyrus the military task of subduing nations (45:1) and setting Israel free from Babylonian Exile (45:13). But Cyrus did not bring the light of salvation to the Gentiles nor was he "a covenant for the people" Israel (42:6). The one similarity between Cyrus and the Servant is the restoration of dispersed Israel to the land (cf. 49:8–12).

ance and securing protection. The language and concepts are similar to the promises given to the servant Israel in 41:9-10, especially the clauses "I took you . . . I called you. . . . I will strengthen you and help you; I will uphold you with my righteous right hand." The divine faithfulness promised to Israel would similarly be manifested toward the Servant, enabling Him to complete His mission on behalf of both Israel and the nations. The enablement of Yahweh is further described in the verb introductory to the phrases describing the Servant—"I will make you to be . . . "

YAHWEH SUMMARIZES THE SERVANT'S TASK (42:6c-7)

God's call and empowerment of the Servant were for the purpose of enabling Him to accomplish God's will. Therefore Yahweh now summarizes the task in which He will help the Servant. The divinely purposed and predicted performance of the Servant is summarized in three particulars: (1) effecting a new covenant for Israel (v. 6c), (2) being a light for the nations (v. 6d), and (3) delivering blind prisoners (v. 7).

The Servant will effect a New Covenant for Israel (v. 6c). One of the most controversial clauses in this Servant poem is "I . . . will make you to be a covenant for the people" (v. 6c). Odendaal suggests that the various explanations "consist, broadly speaking, of attempts to find a shade of meaning differing from the usual for b^erit ["covenant"] or for 'ām ["people"] and often for both."[47] The three main views of this phrase have been summarized by North:[48] (1) "a covenant people," indicating that the Servant is the nation Israel; (2) "a covenant of the peoples (i.e., nations)," 'am ("people") as a reference to mankind (as in v. 5); and (3) "a covenant of the people (i.e., Israel)." This latter view is preferable because unless the context requires a broader sense (as in v. 5), 'am always refers to Israel as a nation. Delitzsch says that when 'am and gôyim ("nations") stand side by side (as in this verse) they "can only mean Israel and the Gentiles." He adds

47. Odendaal, *Eschatological Expectation*, p. 130.
48. North, *Suffering Servant*, p. 132.

that that interpretation is "put beyond doubt" by the parallel
passage in 49:8 (cf. 49:6), where "a covenant for the people"
clearly refers to Israel as a nation.[49]

In comparison with the next phrase ("and a light for the
Gentiles"), it appears that the Servant is not literally either "a
covenant" or "a light" but one who in some way is a cause,
source, mediator, or dispenser of covenant realities or illuminat-
ing benefits. The figure of speech is probably a metonymy in
which the effect (the covenant) stands for the cause (the covenant
mediator).[50] The Servant is the messianic "messenger of the
covenant" of Malachi 3:1. In short, He is the mediator of the
New Covenant with Israel, elaborated in Jeremiah 31:31–34 and
referred to in numerous other prophetic texts (cf. Isa. 54:10;
55:3; 59:20–21; 61:8; Ezek. 16:60–63).[51]

The Servant will become a light for the Gentiles (v. 6d). Although the poetic parallelism of the two phrases ("a covenant for
the people" and "a light for the Gentiles") could equate "the
people" with "the Gentiles," the context and the parallel passage
in 49:8 indicate that "the people" refers to Israel.[52] The figure
(again a metonymy of effect for cause) pictures the Servant

49. Delitzsch, *Isaiah* 2:179; see also E. A. Speiser, "'People' and 'Nation' of
    Israel," *Journal of Biblical Literature* 79 (1960):157–63. Against the iden-
    tification in verse 6 of the "people" with the "Gentiles" is the fact that in
    Isaiah 40–66 only the plural *'ammim* occurs in synonymous parallelism
    with *gôyim* (Odendaal, *Eschatological Expectation*, pp. 130–31). Odendaal
    also demonstrates the appropriateness of the singular *'ām* in verse 5 to
    describe the peoples of the earth (p. 131).
50. Cf. Bullinger, *Figures of Speech*, pp. 560–62. However, Delitzsch, like a
    number of other scholars, maintains that the Servant is not only the
    medium of the covenant but is also Himself the covenant (*Isaiah* 2:180).
    Odendaal develops the concept of covenant representation by a king who
    establishes a covenant on behalf of the people of his nation (*Eschatological
    Expectation*, pp. 129–34). That concept fits well with both the theocratic
    monarchy of ancient Israel and the royal character of the Isaianic Servant.
51. For a theological treatment of the New Covenant, see J. Dwight Pentecost,
    Things to Come (Findlay, Ohio: Dunham, 1958), pp. 116–28; John F.
    Walvoord, *The Millennial Kingdom* (Grand Rapids: Zondervan, 1959),
    pp. 208–20.
52. The imprisoned captives of verse 7 appear to be Israel in Exile. That is
    affirmed in 49:8b, where "the people" are clearly Israelites who are
    restored politically to the land in 49:8c–12.

bringing a condition of spiritual light, illumination, and salvation to the Gentiles. Isaiah 49:6 strongly suggests that light is virtually equivalent to salvation.[53]

The Servant will deliver blind prisoners (v. 7). The third aspect of the Servant's task[54] is "to open eyes that are blind, to free captives from prison, and to release from the dungeon those who sit in darkness." Two interpretive questions concern the identity of those thus delivered—whether they are Jews, Gentiles, or both—and the connotation of the language describing their condition—whether it is literal or figurative. The association of "blind" with sitting "in darkness" suggests figurative blindness (how many of the captives would be literally blind?). Metaphorical blindness fits the preceding context of metaphorical light (v. 6). Also, the blindness in 42:18-20 is spiritual (cf. 6:9-10; 44:9, 18-20). If the blindness is not literal, it is likely that the "prison" and "dungeon" are also not literal. The imprisonment may refer to the nation in the Babylonian captivity (the prophetic background for Isaiah 40–66),[55] the spiritual blindness being due to idolatry (cf. 40:18-20; 46:5; 48:4-5). The Gentiles were also blinded by idolatry (41:5-7) and so were unable to perceive that Yahweh is the true God and that their idols are worthless (41:25-29).

Such an exilic significance in the passage does not rule out reference to the Servant-Messiah, as the messianic promises and the Davidic covenant could potentially have been fulfilled in the postexilic return (cf. Hag. 2:21-23; Zech. 4:6-10; 6:12). However, due to the incomplete obedience of the nation Israel, the "fulness of time" (Gal. 4:4, KJV) would not arrive for about four more centuries. Even then, the further blindness of the

53. It is worth noting that "light" is associated with "justice" in 51:4-6 and 59:9, so the idea may indicate the conditions among men in which justice is administered.
54. My discussion views the Servant ("you," v. 6) as the subject of the verse's infinitives. It is also possible to regard Yahweh ("I," v. 5) as the subject, the infinitives thus denoting Yahweh's goal to be accomplished through the Servant's mission to Israel and the Gentiles. The verse can also be taken as an explanation of how the Servant is a light to the Gentiles.
55. The "captivity" in Babylon, however, does not necessarily rule out literal "prisons" and "dungeons" (cf. 42:22, 24-25).

national leaders (cf. Matt. 12:22–32) resulted in a postponement (from man's perspective) of the ultimate fulfillment of the messianic deliverance that incorporates "a covenant for the people" and "a light for the Gentiles" into one ultimate fulfillment. As Paul notes, at the Messiah's second advent "the deliverer will come from Zion; he will turn godlessness away from Jacob. And this is my covenant with them when I take away their sins" (Rom. 11:26–27, citing Isa. 59:20–21; 27:9).

YAHWEH PROCURES GLORY FOR HIMSELF (42:8–9)

8"I am the LORD; that is my name!
I will not give my glory to another
or my praise to idols.
9See, the former things have taken place,
and new things I declare;
before they spring into being
I announce them to you."

Yahweh directs glory to Himself by the use of prophecy. The addressees indicated by the plural "you" (v. 9) are the Jewish exiles, who have seen "the former things' take place in the early events of Cyrus's career.

YAHWEH ASSERTS HIS UNIQUE PERSON (42:8)

Yahweh first directs glory to Himself by asserting His uniqueness. He affirms His name: "I am the LORD; that is my name!" Then He asserts His refusal to share His glory: "I will not give my glory to another or my praise to idols" (cf. 48:9–11). Yahweh's intolerance of all rivals is absolute. He will put an end to all idolatry.[56] The glory of which Yahweh is so jealous is that of being recognized and worshiped as sovereign Ruler and righteous Deliverer.

---

56. Cf. the frequent trial speeches against idolatry in Isaiah 40–55 (41:1–7, 21–29; 43:8–13; 44:6–8; 45:20–25).

YAHWEH DIRECTS ATTENTION TO HIS USE OF PREDICTION (42:9)

Contrary to Westermann's view,[57] Isaiah 42:9 draws to a climax the Servant poem and indicates its close relationship to the context. In it Yahweh directs attention to His use of predictive prophecy, namely, that just as the first predictions ("the former things") have been fulfilled, even so new predictions that will likewise be fulfilled—the prophecies concerning the messianic Servant—are now being declared.

"The former things" are neither the Exodus from Egypt (cf. Isa. 43:14–20) nor the fall of Babylon (predicted in Isa. 13:17–22; Jer. 51:11, 28–29),[58] but the predictions of the deliverance of Israel from exile by the early events of Cyrus's career. Isaiah's perspective has changed since 41:22, where the "former things" are identified with "what is going to happen."[59] The "new things" are the conditions associated with the righteous order that the messianic Servant will cause to prevail on the whole earth.

CONCLUSION

The anonymous Servant of Isaiah 42:1–9 can be neither Israel nor Cyrus nor any person other than the royal Davidic Messiah, the Lord Jesus Christ. The first Servant song introduces the Servant and highlights the successful completion of the task to which He is divinely called. Only a hint is given of the pathway of suffering that the Servant must tread to arrive at the glory of a completed mission, when He will have caused a righteous order to prevail on the earth. He will bring in a just order on the earth following His second advent at the time of the fulfillment of the promised new covenant for the nation Israel. Gentiles also will benefit from the worldwide blessings of that covenant and kingdom.

57. Westermann says that verse 9 "has no connection with what precedes" (*Isaiah 40–66*, p. 98).
58. Pieper, *Isaiah II*, p. 191; and H. C. Leupold, *Exposition of Isaiah* (Grand Rapids: Baker, 1971), p. 66, respectively.
59. Contra Odendaal, *Eschatological Expectation*, pp. 110–11.

3

The Commission
of the Servant:
Isaiah 49:1–13

In the first Servant song (Isa. 42:1–9) Yahweh conveyed a distant prophecy of His Servant who will bring salvation and establish a proper order on the entire earth. The passage introduced the Servant and promised His faithfulness in accomplishing the mission to which He was divinely called. Scarcely a hint was given of the path of suffering to be trodden by the Servant on the way to His completed mission. The task itself involved mediating a new covenant with Israel and causing a just order to prevail on the whole Gentile world. I concluded that the anonymous Servant of Isaiah 42:1–9 is the royal Davidic Messiah, the Lord Jesus Christ, who will cause a right order to prevail on the earth following His second advent at the time of the fulfillment of the promised new covenant for the nation Israel. In the millennial kingdom worldwide spiritual blessings will extend not only to Israel but also to the Gentiles.

The second Servant song (Isa. 49:1–13) brings out the same basic concepts as the first poem, though the establishment of a worldwide righteous order is not stressed. Instead, greater emphasis is placed on the physical and spiritual restoration of the nation Israel. The primary new feature in the second song is the apparent initial failure of the Servant in His mission to Israel, which brings about an expanded commission from Yahweh to bring salvation to the Gentiles.

The second Servant song begins a new division (49:1—57:21) in Isaiah's Book of Comfort (chaps. 40–66). It is noteworthy that this division also contains the remaining Servant songs (50:4-11; 52:13—53:12). Contrary to much critical opinion,[1] the Servant Songs seem to form the backbone of the structure of this division. Each song begins a cycle that culminates in a powerful message of salvation.[2] For example, the cycle that begins with this second song culminates in the proclamation of salvation to Israel regarding future restoration (49:14-26), a prominent theme in the song itself (49:8–12).

The message of the second song is that the rejected Servant will bring salvation to the Gentiles and ultimately will restore Israel to the land and to Yahweh. The passage emphasizes not only the Servant's expanded commission to the Gentiles but also His ultimate success in fulfilling His initial mission to Israel. Whereas Yahweh was the speaker throughout the first song (42:1-9), the initial strophe of the second song (49:1-6) is a prophetic report by the Servant, followed by two proclamations of salvation (v. 7; vv. 8–12) in which Yahweh addresses the Servant, climaxed by an eschatological hymn by the prophet (v. 13). In the second Servant poem (1) the Servant reports to the nations that Yahweh has expanded His ministry to the Gentiles in view of His rejection by Israel (49:1-6); (2) Yahweh promises His Servant that He will bring to completion both the Gentile and Jewish aspects of the Servant's mission (49:7-12); and (3) the prophet calls on all creation to praise Yahweh, who thus comforts His people (49:13).

THE SERVANT REPORTS HIS EXPANDED MISSION TO THE GENTILES (49:1-6)

¹Listen to me, you islands;
   hear this you distant nations:

1. E.g., Claus Westermann, *Isaiah 40–66: A Commentary* (Philadelphia: Westminster, 1975), pp. 20–21, 29.
2. Robert B. Chisolm, "Toward a Form Critical/Structural Analysis of Isaiah" (student paper, Dallas Theological Seminary, 1980), pp. 62–63.

Before I was born the LORD called me;
　　from my birth he has made mention of my name.
²He made my mouth like a sharpened sword,
　　in the shadow of his hand he hid me;
he made me into a polished arrow
　　and concealed me in his quiver.
³He said to me, "You are my servant,
　　Israel, in whom I will display my splendor."
⁴But I said, "I have labored to no purpose;
　　I have spent my strength in vain and for nothing.
Yet what is due me is in the LORD's hand,
　　and my reward is with my God."
⁵And now the LORD says—
　　he who formed me in the womb to be his
　　　　servant
to bring Jacob back to him
　　and gather Israel to himself,
for I am honored in the eyes of the LORD
　　and my God has been my strength—
⁶he says:
"It is too small a thing for you to be my servant
to restore the tribes of Jacob
　　and bring back those of Israel I have kept.
I will also make you a light for the Gentiles,
　　that you may bring my salvation to the ends of
　　　　the earth."

The Servant reports to the nations His expanded commission by Yahweh to minister to them in view of His rejection by Israel. R. N. Whybray thinks that the literary genre of this paragraph belongs to the "general category of the prophetic call narrative . . . in which the prophet seeks to authenticate his claim to speak on God's behalf"[3] (cf. Amos 7:14–15). In that vein James Muilenburg lists several points of similarity between the prophetic call of Jeremiah and this report of the call of the Servant[4] (cf. Jer. 1:5). Roy F. Melugin, however, appears correct

3. R. N. Whybray, *Isaiah 40–66* (Grand Rapids: Eerdmans, 1981), p. 137.
4. James Muilenburg, "The Book of Isaiah: Chapters 40–66," in *The Interpreter's Bible*, ed. George A. Buttrick (Nashville: Abingdon, 1956), 5:566.

in affirming that "the poem does not make it clear whether it is the commissioning of a prophet or of a king or of some other kind of official."[5]

The development of the paragraph indicates that: (1) the Servant directs attention to His call, preparation, preservation, and commission by Yahweh (vv. 1-3); (2) the Servant makes reference to His past confession of apparent failure and to His past (or present?) affirmation of trust in God (v. 4); and (3) the Servant relates the enlargement of His call to bring salvation to the Gentiles (vv. 5-6).

THE SERVANT SPEAKS OF HIS DIVINE CALL AND COMMISSION (49:1-3)

The Servant announces to the nations His prenatal call by Yahweh (v. 1). The Servant introduces the announcement of His prenatal call by Yahweh with a summons to the nations—"Listen to me, you islands; hear this you distant nations" (v. 1a)—for "the servant speaks with absolute authority, commanding the world to listen."[6] The speaker ("me") is the Servant of verse 6, identical with the Servant of 42:1-9.[7] The worldwide Gentile audience is addressed as "islands"[8] and "distant nations." The Servant then refers to His prenatal call: "Before I was born the LORD called me; from my birth he has made mention of my name" (v. 1b). The Hebrew employs vivid imagery in speaking of the process of birth. The phrases could be translated literally "from the womb" and "from the belly of my mother." E. J. Young over-optimistically suggests, "It is the reference to 'my

---

5. Roy F. Melugin, *The Formation of Isaiah 40-55* (New York: Walter de Gruyter, 1976), p. 143.

6. Edward J. Young, *The Book of Isaiah: The English Text, with Introduction, Exposition, and Notes* (Grand Rapids: Eerdmans, 1965-72), 3:268.

7. The portraits of the Servant in 42:1-9 and 49:1-6 have the following characteristics in common: (1) they picture the Servant in terms of an individual; (2) they view the Servant as distinct from Israel; (3) they describe the Servant's mission to Israel; and (4) they affirm the Servant's broader worldwide mission to the Gentiles.

8. "Islands" refers to "the distant shores of the West [i.e., the Mediterranean basin], representative of all remote areas of the then-known world" (H. C. Leupold, *Exposition of Isaiah* [Grand Rapids: Baker, 1971], 2:63).

mother' that makes it clear that the speaker is the Messiah." Yet, in view of the New Testament truth of the virgin birth of Christ (cf. Matt. 1:18–25), it is appropriate that there is no mention of Messiah's human father in the Old Testament (cf. Gen. 3:15; Ps. 22:9). The idea of calling before birth clearly indicates sovereign choice, but to say that such calling is equivalent with predestination (i.e., pretemporal, rather than just prenatal choice) is a theological rather than an exegetical decision that may or may not be implied in this text. "He has made mention of my name" is literally "He caused my name to be remembered." It is not so much a naming process as a designating event, pointing to the Servant's office and vocation.[9]

The Servant affirms His preparation and preservation by Yahweh (v. 2). The first and third lines of this verse employ synonymous parallelism to indicate the preparation of the Servant: "He made my mouth like a sharpened sword" (simile); "he made me into a polished arrow" (metaphor). The connotation of preparation is seen in that Yahweh "made" the Servant those things. Sharpening and polishing also imply a process of preparation. Similarly, it is possible to speak of the Servant's gifts in terms of His speaking ability. The Servant's "mouth" is probably a metonymy for his words, which are described under the figure of a sharpened sword as cutting or effective. The Servant functions as "the mouthpiece of Yahweh."[10] Christopher R. North thus maintains that "the 'sharp' word [sic] of the Servant is the word of a prophet rather than the edict of a king." Thus "the word of the LORD is a formidable weapon, and it is because the Servant's task is arduous and dangerous that Yahweh does not send him to it until he has been properly equipped to face it."[11] The "polished arrow" is a less common figure (cf. Jer. 23:29), but it seems to indicate either the piercing or the far-ranging effect of the Servant's prophetic word: "God has endowed the Servant's word

9. Young, *Book of Isaiah*, 3:268.
10. Whybray, *Isaiah 40–66*, p. 137.
11. Christopher R. North, *The Second Isaiah: Introduction, Translation, and Commentary to Chapters XL–LV* (Oxford: Clarendon, 1964), p. 187.

with the power to penetrate (a 'sharp sword') and to range far and wide ('a polished arrow')."[12]

The second and fourth lines of verse 2—"in the shadow of his hand he hid me . . . and concealed me in his quiver"—further indicate the Servant's relationship to Yahweh, who prepared Him by preserving Him. But a question arises as to the purpose of the preservation. Is it concealment until the proper time? Or does it simply indicate God's care and protection? If the former, it might refer to the period of over thirty years in Jesus' preparation for public ministry[13] or to His present session in heaven during the interadvent period as He awaits the second advent (cf. Rev. 1:16, where He is described as having a sharp sword coming out of His mouth). On the other hand "to be hidden by the Lord means to be under his care and protection (cf. Psalms 17:8; 27:5; 31:20; 64:2; Jer. 36:26)."[14] Perhaps both elements—concealment as well as protection—are included in Yahweh's preservation of the Servant.

The Servant reports His divine commission as the true Israel to glorify Yahweh (v. 3). In addition to announcing His divine call, preparation, and preservation, the Servant continues His report to the Gentiles with a rehearsal of the words of divine commission. "He said to me, 'You are my servant, Israel, in whom I will display my splendor.'" The literary genre seems to shift at this point from the call of the prophet to the designation of a king (cf. Isa. 42:1–4; Ps. 2:7) But that involves no inconsistency, because the promises concerning the Davidic Messiah (beginning in 2 Sam. 7) and the prophet like Moses (Deut. 18:15), which ultimately merge in the person of Jesus Christ, already begin to intertwine in Isaiah's Servant Songs.

On the surface, the statement "You are my servant, Israel," explicitly identifies Yahweh's Servant as the nation Israel (cf. 41:8–16; 42:18–25; 43:1–13; 44:1–4; 48:20–21). But if that

12. Westermann, *Isaiah 40–66*, p. 208.
13. T. R. Birks, *Commentary on the Book of Isaiah* (London: Rivingtons, 1871), p. 250.
14. Page H. Kelley, "Isaiah," in *The Broadman Bible Commentary*, ed. C. J. Allen (Nashville: Broadman, 1971), 5:330; cf. Westermann, *Isaiah 40–66*, p. 208.

were the case, an apparent contradiction would arise in verses 5–6, in which the Servant's task is to bring Israel back to Yahweh and to the land. That apparent contradiction leads Page H. Kelley to exclaim: "The elusiveness of the Servant's identity is nowhere more apparent than in this second Servant Song."[15]

Some scholars remove the problem by removing the term "Israel" from the text in verse 3. Claus Westermann, for example, regards "Israel" as "a later addition" to the text, "the ancient witness to the collective interpretation of the Servant, one gloss among the many that seek to interpret the text."[16] But this view is contradicted by the manuscript evidence, which clearly supports retention of the term "Israel."[17]

Those who retain "Israel" in the text normally follow one of two interpretive paths: (1) "Israel" means the nation, which in this passage is pictured corporately under the figure of an individual servant, or (2) an individual servant is here designated by the generic name "Israel." North advocates the first view and says that "Israel [v. 3] could have a mission to Israel [vv. 5–6] very much as we say that the first mission of the Church is to the Church."[18] But, as H. C. Leupold responds, "this seems too much like exhorting a nation to draw itself up by its own bootstraps."[19] Furthermore, the vivid detail in the description of the Servant as an individual "goes beyond possibilities of metaphor"[20] (e.g., the expression "from the bowels of my mother," v. 1, KJV).

The view of Edward J. Young that "*Israel* then is a description of the true people of God, the whole body of the redeemed as members under the Head, the Messiah," is just as deficient as the similar view of Joseph A. Alexander.[21] T. R. Birks refuted

15. Kelley, "Isaiah," p. 329.
16. Westermann, *Isaiah 40–66*, p. 209.
17. North, *Second Isaiah*, pp. 187–88.
18. Ibid., p. 189.
19. Leupold, *Exposition of Isaiah*, 2:175.
20. Whybray, *Isaiah 40–66*, p. 136.
21. Young, *Book of Isaiah* 3:270. Joseph A. Alexander interprets "Israel" as a "complex subject including the Messiah and his people," i.e., the Christian church (*Commentary on the Prophecies of Isaiah* [Grand Rapids: Zondervan, 1953], 2:226).

that view over a century ago as "opposed to the plain words of the text. . . . For the Church is not a single person, has no mother, was not named by prophecy before birth, does not restore Israel, is the receiver, not the giver of salvation."[22] Thus the view that "Israel" (49:3) is a title of the individual messianic Servant harmonizes most satisfactorily with the passage and context.[23]

The glorification of Yahweh in His Servant is indicated as the ultimate purpose in the commission of the Servant: "in whom I will display my splendor." While the Servant speaks in verse 5 of His honor and success in the eyes of Yahweh, in verse 3 Yahweh directs attention to the Servant's glorification. Westermann avers that it is expected of a servant to glorify his master, not of the master to glorify the servant, and views the glorification as "a hidden and paradoxical one; partly because the lord's [sic] purpose is to glorify himself at the hands of the Servant, and partly because only the opposite of glory can be discerned in the Servant."[24] The ultimate resolution of the paradox is discerned in the distinction between the Servant's accomplishments at His two advents, the first advent culminating in "the sufferings of Christ" and the second advent manifesting "the glories that would follow" (1 Pet. 1:11). That glorification is manifested in part by the Servant's ultimate acceptance by Gentile kings and princes (Isa. 49:7).

22. Birks, Commentary, p. 250.
23. The words of Franz J. Delitzsch are significant at this point: "Israel was from the very first the God-given name of an individual. Just as the name Israel was first of all given to a man, and then after that to a nation, so the name which sprang from a personal root has also a personal crown" (Isaiah, Commentary on the Old Testament [Grand Rapids: Eerdmans, 1973], 2:260). David F. Payne concludes, "Verse 3 entitles this coming Servant 'Israel' who will bring glory to God, in marked contrast to the historical Israel" ("Isaiah," in The New Layman's Bible Commentary, ed. G. C. D. Howley, F. F. Bruce, and H. L. Ellison [Grand Rapids: Zondervan, 1979], p. 805). H. S. Nyberg regards the name "Israel" as a title of honor, inasmuch as "a nation's ancestor, living on in his descendants, can be especially associated with the leader or king as the current head and 'father'" (cf. 2 Sam. 19:44; 1 Kings 12:16) (cited by John H. Eaton, Festal Drama in Deutero-Isaiah [London: S.P.C.K., 1979], pp. 63–64).
24. Westermann, Isaiah 40–66, pp. 209–10.

THE SERVANT CONFESSES HIS APPARENT FAILURE
BUT AFFIRMS HIS FAITH IN GOD (49:4)

This verse is a present acknowledgment by the Servant of His past confession of apparent failure and of His past (or present?) affirmation of trust in God. It possibly reflects several motifs of the thanksgiving or declarative praise psalm.[25] Westermann calls it a "lament of a mediator."[26] It is not clear whether the confession of trust (v. 4b) is a part of the past lament (the NIV includes it within the quotation that follows "I said") or is a present statement in contrast to the past lament. In either case the context implies a continuing confidence in God on the part of the Servant.

The Servant reports His apparent past failure (v. 4a). The Servant's affirmation of confidence in God (v. 4b) comes in the wake of His reference to apparent failure regarding the fruitfulness of His mission to Israel (cf. v. 5). "But I said, 'I have labored to no purpose; I have spent my strength in vain and for nothing.'" Though these words may reflect discouragement and despondency on the part of the Servant, they do not reflect doubt or defeat, for the Servant retains His confidence in Yahweh despite difficulties (cf. Isa. 42:4; Ps. 22). The adversative "but" contrasts the high calling and remarkable abilities of the Servant (vv. 1–3) with His seemingly disappointing results in carrying out His task (v. 4a). The passage is reminiscent of the situation of Jeremiah, the weeping prophet (cf. Jer. 15:10, 18; 20:14–18). The fulfillment of this passage appears to be the progressive rejection of Christ by Israel, which culminated in His death on the cross (cf. Matt. 12:9–37; 23:37–39; 26:1—27:66).

The Servant affirms His confidence in God (v. 4b). The Servant's apparent failure does not abort His expression of confidence in God. "Yet what is due me is in the LORD's hand [lit., "my right is with Yahweh"], and my reward is with my God" (v. 4b). The word translated "what is due me" (NIV) or "my

25. For example, the declarative praise psalm reports a past lament before declaring God's delivering actions. See Claus Westermann, *The Praise of God in the Psalms* (Richmond, Virg.: John Knox, 1965), pp. 102–16.
26. Westermann, *Isaiah 40–66*, pp. 210.

judgment" (KJV) is from מִשְׁפָּט (*mishpāṭ*), the word so significant
in the first Servant song. It is tempting to translate and interpret
mishpāṭ here in a sense identical with its usage in 42:1, 3, 4,
where it refers to the Servant's activity in establishing a just order
on the whole earth.[27] But it is probably "best to preserve the
judicial sense of משפט *mishpāṭ* that the verdict of Yahweh on the
service of the Servant will be a favorable one."[28] Thus "vindication" (or "just reward") would be an appropriate translation.
The parallel with פְּעֻלָּתִי (*pe'ullātî*), meaning "reward" or "recom-
pense" (i.e., the fruit or result of His labor; cf. Lev. 19:13; Prov.
10:16; 11:18; Isa. 61:8), supports that meaning. In further support of that view, August Pieper points out that "the suffix [the
pronoun "my" in English] shows that this right is a personal
prerogative of the Servant."[29] In contrast with the apparent failure
of His mission, the Servant voices His deepest trust that Yahweh
will confirm and vindicate His work by granting His Servant
ultimate success (cf. Isa. 50:8; 53:11–12). Although the dark
shadow of the cross apparently blacks out the accomplishment
of God's purpose, the brilliant splendor of the crown reflects the
ultimate success of the Servant.

THE SERVANT RELATES HIS ENLARGED CALL TO BRING SALVATION
TO THE GENTILES (49:5–6)

    Rather than resulting in the discontinuation of His mission,
the apparent failure of the Servant leads to an enlargement of His
mission to include all nations. Although the Gentile mission of
the Servant is an advancement in the task of the Servant to
glorify God and follows on His rejection by the Jews (cf. Acts
13:47), the enlarged task neither annuls nor changes God's purpose for Israel to be fulfilled through the Servant.
    The Servant affirms Yahweh's purpose to restore Israel spiritu-

27. E.g., Allan A. MacRae, *The Gospel of Isaiah* (Chicago: Moody, 1977),
    p. 106.
28. Scott Rae, "An Exegetical and Theological Study of Isaiah 49:1–13"
    (Th.M. thesis, Dallas Theological Seminary, 1981), p. 37; cf. North,
    Second Isaiah, pp. 188–89.
29. August Pieper, *Isaiah II: An Exposition of Isaiah 40–66* (1919; trans.,
    Milwaukee: Northwestern, 1979), p. 355.

ally through Him (v. 5). Before rehearsing the enlarged call ("And now the LORD says . . .") concerning the Gentile mission, the Servant recapitulates and evidently reaffirms Yahweh's initial calling and purpose to bring salvation to Israel: "He who formed me in the womb to be his servant to bring Jacob back to him and gather Israel again to himself, for I am honored in the eyes of the LORD and my God has been my strength." Westermann justifiably calls verse 5 "a longish introduction" to the new commission in verse 6.[30] The emphasis on the originally revealed purpose of God through the Servant does not speak of its nonfulfillment but rather reaffirms its ultimate fulfillment. The Servant was born to accomplish a certain divine purpose, and the power of God through the Servant will not fail in the accomplishment of that purpose. Allan A. MacRae's suggestion that the phrase "formed me in the womb" possibly refers to the virgin birth[31] must be evaluated in the light of one's conclusion regarding the similar reference to the birth process in verse 1.

The purpose of the Servant's mission as stated in this verse is *spiritual*: to bring Israel back to God Himself (cf. Isa. 55:7; Jer. 4:1), not to bring them back from Babylon.[32] The Hebrew text (i.e., Kethiv) has the negative לֹא (*lō'*), "not" (KJV), which has the same sound as the Qere לוֹ (*lô*), "to himself" (NIV and other modern translations). Probably לוֹ (*lô*) is to be preferred, having the support of 1QIs[a] and some other manuscripts and versions. The resulting synonymous parallelism between "bring back to him" and "gather to himself" also gives a smoother understanding of the passage. However, if לֹא (*lō'*) is correct, then the verb probably has the sense of "sweep away": "that Israel might not be swept away."[33]

The verse concludes with an assurance of the Servant's vindication before Yahweh, probably anticipating His ultimate success in His mission to Israel.

The Servant affirms Yahweh's enlarged call (v. 6). The Servant

---

30. Westermann, *Isaiah 40–66*, p. 211.
31. MacRae, *Gospel of Isaiah*, p. 106.
32. Young, *Book of Isaiah*, 3:273–74; Young correctly notes that the Servant rather than Yahweh is the subject of the infinitive (p. 273, n. 10).
33. Whybray, *Isaiah 40–66*, p. 139; North, *Second Isaiah*, pp. 185–86.

affirms Yahweh's enlarged call not only for the Servant to restore Israel physically to the land but also to bring salvation to the Gentiles spiritually. The Servant first quotes Yahweh's commission to Him regarding an enlarged mission to the Gentiles. Yahweh answers the Servant's discouragement (v. 4a) with a call to greater responsibility (cf. Jer. 12:5; 15:19–21; 1 Kings 19:9–18). The enlarged task is related to the initial task regarding Israel: "It is too small a thing for you to be my servant to restore the tribes of Jacob and bring back those of Israel I have kept" (v. 6a).

The phrase "tribes of Jacob" implies political organization and so a political task, that is, restoring the tribes of Jacob back to the position of dignity they do not now enjoy.[34] As verse 5 identified the spiritual aspect of the Servant's task toward Israel— to bring Israel back to God—so this verse indicates the physical/ political aspect of the mission—to bring Israel back to the land. Yet even that is "too small a thing," that is, it is insignificant in comparison with the greater task of bringing salvation to the whole world. That neither belittles nor annuls the Servant's mission to Israel, but enlarges it. "The greater task . . . does not exclude the lesser."[35] Yahweh promises the Servant success in both His Jewish and Gentile missions (49:6–12).

Young sees that work of restoration as being first the return from exile and finally "the spiritual restoration of [spiritual] Israel [i.e., in the church] accomplished by Christ." His conclusion that "nowhere does the Bible teach that the entire physical Israel will be saved"[36] cannot be harmonized with a proper understanding of Romans 11:26–27. At the second-advent judgment on living Israelites (described in Matt. 25:1–30; Ezek. 20:37–38; Mal. 3:2–3, 5), the unbelievers will be purged out of Israel through physical death, leaving on earth a regenerate nation Israel (along with regenerate Gentiles) at the beginning of the millennial kingdom.[37]

34. But contrast Young, Book of Isaiah, 3:275.
35. Ibid.; but Young does not see the lesser task as the physical restoration of Israel.
36. Ibid.
37. See John F. Walvoord, The Millennial Kingdom (Grand Rapids: Zondervan, 1973), pp. 186–93.

The enlarged mission to the Gentiles climaxes the Servant's commission from Yahweh: "I will also make you a light for the Gentiles, that you may bring my salvation to the ends of the earth" (v. 6*b*). "Light" is here parallel with "salvation" (cf. Isa. 42:6). Yahweh's initiative is clearly indicated in the verb ("I will also make you"), as is seen by Young: "God has appointed the servant to this work and determined that he should carry it out."[38]

YAHWEH PROMISES A COMPLETELY FULFILLED MISSION TO THE SERVANT (49:7-12)

⁷This is what the LORD says—
     the Redeemer and Holy One of Israel—
to him who was despised and abhorred by the nation,
     to the servant of rulers:
"Kings will see you and arise,
     princes will see you and bow down,
because of the LORD, who is faithful,
     the Holy One of Israel, who has chosen you."
⁸This is what the LORD says:
"In the time of my favor I will answer you,
     and in the day of salvation I will help you;
I will keep you and will make you
     to be a covenant for the people,
to restore the land
     and to assign its desolate inheritances,
⁹to say to the captives, 'Come out,'
     and to those in darkness, 'Be free!'
They will feed beside the roads
     and find pasture on every barren hill.
¹⁰They will neither hunger nor thirst,
     nor will the desert heat or the sun beat upon them.
He who has compassion on them will guide them
     and lead them beside springs of water.
¹¹I will turn all my mountains into roads,
     and my highways will be raised up.
¹²See, they will come from afar—

38. Young, *Book of Isaiah*, 3:276.

some from the north, some from the west,
some from the region of Sinim."

The speaker in this section is Yahweh (v. 7*a*), the person addressed is the Servant (v. 7*b*),[39] and the subject is the ultimate success of the Servant with respect to both Israel and the Gentiles. Yahweh promises to His Servant that He will fulfill both the Gentile and Jewish aspects of the Servant's mission: that the Gentiles will worship Him (v. 7) and that Israel will be restored by Him (vv. 8–12). That twofold fulfillment of the Servant's mission (Gentile and Jewish aspects) corresponds with the literary genre of the passage, which consists of two oracles, or announcements, of salvation, one concerning the worship of the Gentiles (v. 7) and the other regarding the restoration of Israel (vv. 8–12). Thus the development is twofold: (1) Yahweh promises His despised Servant that the Gentiles will worship Him (v. 7); and (2) Yahweh promises His Servant that at the appointed time He will restore Israel in safety from all over the earth (vv. 8–12).

YAHWEH PROMISES HIS DESPISED SERVANT
THAT THE GENTILES WILL WORSHIP HIM (49:7)

The messenger formula that introduces this announcement of salvation is expanded (cf. 42:5) with two divine titles: "This is what the LORD says—the Redeemer and Holy One of Israel" (v. 7*a*). Those two titles are often combined by Isaiah (cf. 41:14; 43:14; 47:4; 48:17; 49:7; 54:5). The term גֹּאֵל (*gō'ēl*, "Redeemer"), customarily referred to a near kinsman who protected a distressed relative in various circumstances[40] (e.g., Lev. 25:47–49; Num. 35:19; Ruth 3:11–13). Isaiah often uses it figuratively of Yahweh's intimate and binding relationship to Israel. The title

---

39. The "Servant" in 49:7–12 is not Israel (contra Westermann, *Isaiah 40–66*, p. 214; Whybray, *Isaiah 40–66*, p. 140), although North asserts that this passage has been claimed as a Servant song less often than 42:5–9 (*Second Isaiah*, p. 191). The view taken in this book is that both 42:5–9 and 49:7–12 are developments within their respective Servant songs.
40. See the discussion of Yahweh as *gō'ēl* in chapter 1.

"Holy One of Israel" indicates that the God who judges Israel (cf. Isa. 1:4) is the same God who redeems Israel.

Yahweh addresses the Servant in words that show the completeness of Israel's rejection of Him: "to him who was despised and abhorred by the nation, to the servant of rulers" (v. 7b). The *New International Version* incorporates the term נֶפֶשׁ (*nepesh*, "soul"), into the verb. "Despised of soul" could mean "despised in regard to his soul," that is, deemed unworthy to live, or "despised from the soul," that is, heartily despised.[41] If *nepesh* is rather taken to mean "people" (cf. Gen. 17:14), then the translation "despised of men" would parallel both Isaiah 53:3 and the parallel phrases here in 49:7 ("abhorred by the nation" and "servant of rulers"). The word גּוֹי (*gôy*, "nation"), probably does not refer to "the human race generally"[42] but rather to the nation Israel. The "rulers" could refer to both Jewish and Gentile leaders who reject Him before the ultimate success of His mission.

The Servant will ultimately be recognized and worshiped by Gentile kings: "Kings will see you and arise, princes will see and bow down" (v. 7c). That recognition of the Servant for what He actually is anticipates 52:15. The reversal of the Servant's circumstances (from rejection to recognition in worship) depends on the faithfulness of Yahweh: "because of the LORD, who is faithful, the Holy One of Israel, who has chosen you" (v. 7d).

YAHWEH PROMISES TO RESTORE ISRAEL
AT THE APPOINTED TIME (49:8–12)

Yahweh's promise to restore Israel through His Servant is perplexing to scholars such as North, who says, "This looks very much like the political task which Yahweh had said he no longer requires of the Servant."[43] The solution does not lie in the deletion or transposition of certain lines of the text, as done by North,[44] but rather in the recognition that God is not finished

41. So Whybray, *Isaiah 40–66*, p. 141; Young, *Book of Isaiah*, 3:276–77.
42. Delitzsch, *Isaiah*, 2:264.
43. North, *Second Isaiah*, p. 191.
44. Ibid.

blessing Israel as a nation even though she was involved in the initial rejection of the Servant.

Yahweh promises His Servant help in restoring Israel (49:8). The keynote of the paragraph is struck as Yahweh ("This is what the LORD says") promises His Servant help in restoring Israel at the appointed time. "In the time of my favor I will answer you, and in the day of salvation I will help you; I will keep you and will make you to be a covenant for the people, to restore the land and to reassign its desolate inheritances." The verbs "answer" and "help" probably imply a previous lament by the Servant (as alluded to in v. 4a; cf. Ps. 22:19-21). The temporal nouns "time" and "day" indicate not the time limits but the certainty of the events to be accomplished. Whybray regards the clause "I will keep you and will make you to be a covenant for the people" as a later addition from 42:6 (where he thinks it refers to Cyrus). As evidence he suggests that because the context (49:8-12) is "wholly concerned with the restoration of Israel," the phrase "a covenant for the people" is unfitting.[45] But that argument presupposes that "the people" עַם ('am) are Gentiles rather than Israel. As indicated in the exposition of 42:6-7, the phrase "a covenant for the people" refers to Yahweh's new covenant with His people Israel, which He will establish through His Servant-Messiah. The same truth is repeated here in the context of Israel's future restoration to the land, thus combining the spiritual blessings of the new covenant for Israel with the physical blessings of her restoration to the land.

Leupold approaches the promise of restoration differently, by limiting its fulfillment to the period of Jewish restoration from Babylon: "This means that the Restoration from Captivity in particular will be brought about by the Messiah. Strangely, before his Incarnation he brings blessings to his people."[46] It is better to view the incarnation of the coming messianic Servant as imminent (but unfulfilled) during the period of the return from Babylon. Delitzsch, for example, sees the prophet Isaiah as foreseeing Yahweh's Servant in the time of the Assyrian oppres-

---

45. Whybray, Isaiah 40-66, p. 141.
46. Leupold, Exposition of Isaiah, 2:181.

sions, "rising up in the second half of the captivity, as if born in exile, in the midst of the punishment borne by his people, to effect the restoration of Israel."[47] Young asserts concerning the restoration in verse 8, "The picture refers primarily not to the return from exile, but to the reestablishment of the Davidic kingdom under the Messiah, when all the true seed of Abraham will receive their promised inheritance."[48] Unfortunately, by "all the true seed of Abraham" Young means believers during the present church age. If he were to mean those regenerate Jews at the second advent to whom the new covenant will be fulfilled (cf. Rom. 11:26–27), it would be an excellent statement of the meaning of this passage. The "desolate inheritances" relate to the physical land of Israel (cf. Isa. 1:7; 6:11; 17:9; 54:1; 61:4; 62:4; 64:10). Thus the promise of Israel's final and permanent restoration to the land (cf. Amos 9:11-15) awaits fulfillment following the return of the Servant-Messiah.

Yahweh promises that the Servant will regather His captive people (v. 9a). Yahweh's promise to help His Servant restore Israel at the appointed time (v. 8) includes the promise that the Servant will regather Yahweh's captive people: "to say to the captives, 'Come out,' and to those in darkness, 'Be free!'" Although the language of this promise may be taken from the Exile (as anticipated by Isaiah), the ultimate fulfillment in the context relates to the future day when the messianic Servant will establish the new covenant with Israel at His return (cf. Isa. 42:7).

Yahweh promises that the Servant will shepherd His needy flock (vv. 9b–10). The imagery of the promise indicates that the Servant will shepherd Yahweh's needy flock. "They will feed beside the roads and find pasture on every barren hill. They will neither hunger nor thirst, nor will the desert heat or the sun beat upon them. He who has compassion on them will guide them and lead them beside springs of water." The language is reminiscent of the Exodus, and it would have been appropriate and could have been fulfilled during the return from the Babylonian Captivity if the Servant had come at that time. It also could have been fulfilled

47. Delitzsch, *Isaiah*, 2:258-59.
48. Young, *Book of Isaiah*, 3:279.

when the Messiah did come, in the Herodian period of the first-century Roman Empire, but the rejection of the Servant at that time has delayed its fulfillment (from the human perspective) until the second advent.

Yahweh promises to regather His people from all over the earth *(vv. 11–12).* The promise concludes that Yahweh's people will be marshaled from great distances and all directions on the earth. The figure appears to be changed from that of the shepherd and his sheep to that of a great people on the march. "I will turn all my mountains into roads, and my highways will be raised up. See, they will come from afar—some from the north, some from the west, some from the region of Sinim." An ancient interpretation links "Sinim" with China—a view that still has many adherents.[49] Whybray represents many modern scholars who identify it as modern Aswan, a district on the southern frontier of ancient Egypt.[50]

Regardless of the exact location of that area, the thrust of the promise is that Yahweh will remove all obstacles that hinder the return of His people Israel to their land from all over the earth.

ISAIAH CALLS ON ALL CREATION TO PRAISE YAHWEH (49:13)

> [13]Shout for joy, O heavens;
>   rejoice, O earth;
>   burst into song, O mountains!
> For the LORD comforts his people
>   and will have compassion on his afflicted ones.

The prophet Isaiah has communicated the Servant's report of His expanded mission to the Gentiles (vv. 1–6) and Yahweh's promise to the Servant that the Servant will completely fulfill His mission, not only in the expanded Gentile aspect (v. 7) but also in the originally stated purpose of the spiritual and physical restoration of the nation Israel (vv. 7–12). Therefore Isaiah now calls on all creation to praise Yahweh, who thus delivers His

49. MacRae, *Gospel of Isaiah*, pp. 110–11.
50. Whybray, *Isaiah 40–66*, p. 142.

people, because when the nation Israel is properly related to Yahweh, then all creation will rejoice (cf. Isa. 42:10–12; 52:9; 55:12–13).

THE CALL TO PRAISE (49:13*a*)

Isaiah follows the normal structure of the hymnic genre (cf. Ps. 117) by introducing the cause for praise (v. 13*b*) with a preceding call to praise (v. 13*a*): "Shout for joy, O heavens; rejoice, O earth; burst into song, O mountains!" The verbs are characteristic of the vocabulary of praise found in the Psalter.[51] Isaiah's synonymous parallelism characteristically draws the whole universe into singing Yahweh's praise.

THE CAUSE FOR PRAISE (49:13*b*)

Yahweh is worthy of all praise because of His infinite greatness and grace. In this case the cause of praise is His grace toward His people Israel in redeeming them and restoring them to the land. "For the LORD comforts his people and will have compassion on his afflicted ones." The context suggests that the verbs relate to the future when Yahweh will "have compassion on his afflicted ones" as manifested in His redeeming acts, and thus He will comfort His people Israel.

CONCLUSION

Yahweh's called and gifted Servant is rejected at first by His own people Israel, but in a future day of grace He will ultimately succeed not only in fulfilling an expanded mission to bring salvation to the Gentiles but also in restoring Israel both to the land (physically and politically) and to Yahweh (spiritually), thus eliciting universal praise to Yahweh, the Redeemer and Holy One of Israel.

---

51. Ronald Barclay Allen, *Praise! A Matter of Life and Breath* (Nashville: Thomas Nelson, 1980), pp. 64–69.

4

The Commitment
of the Servant:
Isaiah 50:4–11

The first two of Isaiah's Songs of the Servant placed emphasis on the ultimate success of Yahweh's Servant-Messiah. In Isaiah 42:1–9 Yahweh introduced His Servant and predicted the Servant's faithfulness in accomplishing His divinely appointed mission of bringing salvation and establishing a proper order on the whole earth. In the second song (Isa. 49:1–13) a new feature of apparent initial failure by the Servant was introduced, but His ultimate success was predicted not only in fulfilling an expanded mission to bring salvation to the Gentiles but also in restoring Israel both to the land (physically and politically) and to Yahweh (spiritually).

The third Servant song (Isa. 50:4–11)[1] amplifies the sufferings and patient endurance of the Servant, which were only hinted at in the previous songs. All of this is in preparation for the magnum opus of the fourth song (52:13—53:12), in which

---

1. "Although the word 'servant' . . . is not used, the similarity of the passage with the second 'Song,' together with the use of the first person sing., leaves no doubt that it belongs to the same series" (R. N. Whybray, *Isaiah 40–66* [Grand Rapids: Eerdmans, 1981], p. 150).

the Servant-Messiah's suffering and His consequent exaltation are revealed with equal emphasis. "Common to both [the third and fourth songs] is the new conception of the Servant as *sufferer*, here [50:4-9] at the hands of men, there [chap. 53] at the hands of men and God alike."[2] As in the previous songs, the Servant can be neither Isaiah himself (who nowhere else in the book is described as suffering) nor the nation Israel (whose humiliation and sufferings were neither voluntary nor [to anticipate chap. 53] vicarious or substitutionary).[3]

Like the preceding Servant song, the third song begins a cycle that culminates in a powerful message of salvation (51:1—52:12).[4] The short trial speech in Isaiah 50:1-3 forms somewhat of a transition from the preceding Servant-song/salvation-oracle cycle (49:1-26) to the current cycle in 50:4—52:12. In that trial speech Yahweh proves the unreasonableness of His rejection by Israel. The speaker in 50:1-3 is Yahweh, not the Servant.[5] Thus the speech is not part of the Servant song, although some good reasons have been given for regarding all of chapter 50 as a literary unit.[6] The oracle of Yahweh in 50:10-11 is closely connected in thought to the preceding verses, and so it should be included in the third Servant song.

The message of 50:4-11 is fairly clear: The righteous but rejected Servant of Yahweh indicates that Yahweh who discipled Him will also vindicate Him. That is the basis for Yahweh's exhortation for the faithful to walk by faith even in darkness, and His threat to the self-righteous wicked regarding eventual judgment. Except for the wicked who are addressed by Yahweh in verse 11 (and possibly the potential adversaries in v. 8), the primary audience throughout the song seems to be the faithful

2. John Skinner, *The Book of the Prophet Isaiah: Chapters XL—LXVI* (Cambridge: Cambridge U., 1951), p. 113.
3. Allan A. MacRae, *The Gospel of Isaiah* (Chicago: Moody, 1977), p. 119.
4. Likewise, the fourth song (Isa. 52:13—53:12) introduces a message of salvation (54:1-17). Cf. Robert B. Chisolm, "Toward a Form Critical/ Structural Analysis of Isaiah" (student paper, Dallas Theological Seminary, 1980), pp. 62-63.
5. This is in contradistinction to several older interpreters such as T. R. Birks, (*Commentary on the Book of Isaiah* [London: Rivingtons, 1871], p. 256.
6. James Muilenburg, "The Book of Isaiah: Chapters 40-66," in *The Interpreter's Bible*, ed. George A. Buttrick (Nashville: Abingdon, 1956), 5:579.

disciples of Yahweh's Servant, as identified in verse 10. As will be indicated below, the Servant is the speaker in verses 4–9, and Yahweh is the speaker in verses 10–11.[7]

The third Servant song is thus composed of two units: (1) the Servant declares that Yahweh who discipled Him will also vindicate Him (50:4–9); and (2) Yahweh contrasts the obedient walk of the Servant's disciples with the judgment to come on the wicked (50:10–11).

THE SERVANT DECLARES THAT YAHWEH WHO DISCIPLED HIM WILL ALSO VINDICATE HIM (50:4–9)

> [4]The Sovereign LORD has given me an instructed tongue,
> to know the word that sustains the weary.
> He wakens me morning by morning,
> wakens my ear to listen like one being taught.
> [5]The Sovereign LORD has opened my ears,
> and I have not been rebellious;
> I have not drawn back.
> [6]I offered my back to those who beat me,
> my cheeks to those who pulled out my beard;
> I did not hide my face
> from mocking and spitting.
> [7]Because the Sovereign LORD helps me,
> I will not be disgraced.
> Therefore have I set my face like flint,
> and I know I will not be put to shame.
> [8]He who vindicates me is near.
> Who then will bring charges against me?
> Let us face each other!
> Who is my accuser?
> Let him confront me!
> [9]It is the Sovereign LORD who helps me.
> Who is he that will condemn me?

---

7. The literary genre of the Servant's speech and Yahweh's speech will be treated individually.

> They will all wear out like a garment;
> the moths will eat them up.

In this section the righteous but rejected Servant indicates
that Yahweh who has discipled Him will also vindicate Him, and
implies that through His rejection He has learned to comfort the
weary.

Some writers have incorrectly identified this literary unit as
a lament psalm of the individual.[8] Verses 4–6 do have some
resemblance to the lament motif (including the protestation of
innocence), and verse 7 is clearly an expression of confidence
(another lament motif). But the absence of the vital motif of
petition rules out the identity of this song as a lament psalm. It
could more properly be called a psalm of confidence.[9]

The Servant is the speaker, who, as in 49:1–6, appears
without any introduction.[10] The addressees are not identified
except in verse 8, which is a challenge to potential adversaries.
The remaining verses (vv. 4–7, 9) appear to be addressed primarily to the obedient disciples of the Servant (cf. v. 10).

This "autobiographical confession"[11] of the Servant includes two parts: (1) the committed Servant reports His past
obedience and sufferings as the "Disciple" of Yahweh (vv. 4–6),
and (2) the rejected Servant expresses confidence that Yahweh
will vindicate Him (vv. 7–9).

---

8. E.g., J. Begrich, *Studien zu Deuterojesaja* (Munich, 1963), p. 48.
9. Claus Westermann, *Isaiah 40–66: A Commentary* (Philadelphia: Westminster, 1975), pp. 226–28; cf. Ivan Engnell, "The 'Ebed Yahweh Songs
   and the Suffering Messiah in Deutero-Isaiah," *Bulletin of John Rylands
   Library* 31 (January 1948), pp. 70–71. Engnell calls 50:4–9 "a royal
   psalm of confidence" ("'Ebed Yahweh Songs," p. 70), but the Servant
   appears in this passage more in His prophetic role.
10. Henri Blocher recognizes the first-person discourse as supporting an
    individual messianic interpretation: "this kind of I-discourse is found
    nowhere else [than 49:1–6; 50:4–11; 61:1–3] in the entire book of Isaiah.
    When the prophet tells us about events in his own life ... the style,
    mood, and situation are altogether different. The kind of I-discourse
    which we have in the second [and third] Song is found only when God is
    the speaker. God—and the Servant" (*Songs of the Servant* [London: Inter-
    Varsity, 1975], pp. 35–36).
11. Muilenburg, "Book of Isaiah," p. 579.

THE SERVANT REPORTS HIS COMMITMENT TO YAHWEH
WHO DISCIPLED HIM (50:4-6)

*The Servant asserts His role as the Disciple-Prophet of Yahweh
(v. 4).* Before amplifying the daily discipling process whereby
Yahweh taught Him, the Servant states the results of that process:
"The Sovereign LORD has given me an instructed tongue, to know
the word that sustains the weary" (v. 4*a*). It is Adonai Yahweh
("the Sovereign LORD") who has given His Servant the ability to
speak eloquently and encouragingly. This longer title of Yahweh
(occurring four times in this song, always at the beginning of a
verse, cf. vv. 5, 7, 9) calls attention to the sovereign superiority
of Him who disciples the Servant.

The Hebrew word לִמּוּדִים (*limmûdîm*), translated "instructed," occurs again at the end of the verse, where it is
translated "one being taught." Comparable to the English word
"scholar," *limmûdîm* can refer to one in the educational process
("a learner") or to one who has completed or is at least well
advanced in that process ("one who is learned"). E. W. Hengstenberg is representative of those who translate both occurrences
in this verse as "disciple" ("a disciple's tongue" and "a disciple's
ear"), indicating that "He who hears the Lord's words, also
speaks the Lord's words."[12] Other scholars translate the first
occurrence as "an expert tongue," that is, "a tongue adapted to
deliver effectively the message that is given Him to communi-
cate."[13] Care should be taken to avoid a disjunction between the
two occurrences or between the educational process and the
educational product. True, the first use probably identifies "the
Servant's endowment with prophetic eloquence,"[14] but that endowment is made effectual by the daily learning process, which
requires a disciple's ear. As a disciple, the word the Servant
proclaims is not His own—it is a word that He has received from

12. E. W. Hengstenberg, *Christology of the Old Testament and a Commentary
on the Messianic Predictions* (Grand Rapids: Kregal, 1956), 2:251.
13. H. C. Leupold, *Exposition of Isaiah* (Grand Rapids: Baker, 1971), 2:193;
Christopher R. North, *The Second Isaiah: Introduction, Translation, and
Commentary to Chapters XL—LV* (Oxford: Clarendon, 1964), p. 203.
14. Skinner, *Book of the Prophet*, p. 113.

His Teacher (cf. John 17:7–8). Because His teacher is the "Sovereign LORD," the Servant-Disciple enters into the role of a prophet, delivering God's word to "the weary." Claus Westermann correctly concludes that this is "the utterance of a man whose being is governed by hearing and speaking. In both respects he is 'like a disciple,' which means that in both his hearing and his speaking he is concentrated on God, and that these have God as their source."[15]

Although the passage is clearly messianic—fulfilled in the prophetic office of Jesus Christ[16]—it is not the intent of the passage to direct attention to the uniqueness of the Servant (as August Pieper suggests[17]). Instead the purpose is to identify the Servant as a disciple and prophet of Yahweh. Of course, the Messiah-Servant fulfills those functions in a unique manner.

Yahweh schools His Servant so that His Servant will "know the word that sustains the weary." It is experiential knowledge of the divine word that enables the Servant to sustain the weary. The word translated "sustains" עוּת ('ût) is a hapax legomenon. Although many commentators have identified the verb with the word for "time" עֵת ('ēt) and translated it "to speak seasonably,"[18] the translation "sustains" fits smoothly into the passage and may be related to an Arabic root meaning "to help."[19] In Isaiah 40:27–31 the "weary" are Israel. A similar identification here would support the view that the Servant is an individual distinguished from Israel.[20] However, because the Servant's mis-

---

15. Westermann, *Isaiah 40–66*, p. 228.
16. It is noteworthy that the first song describes the Servant's royal characteristics, the second is vague but perhaps combines royal and prophetic aspects, the third song describes His prophetic role, and the fourth song combines aspects of His prophetic and priestly work. Thus the combined picture of the Servant Songs alludes to the threefold office of Christ.
17. August Pieper, *Isaiah II: An Exposition of Isaiah 40–66* (1919; trans., Milwaukee: Northwestern, 1979), p. 388.
18. Joseph A. Alexander, *Commentary on the Prophecies of Isaiah* (Grand Rapids: Zondervan, 1953), 2:250.
19. Cf. North, *Second Isaiah*, p. 201.
20. However, Roy F. Melugin contends, "It would not be unseemly at all for Israel to have a prophetic mission to her own weary" (*The Formation of Isaiah 40–55* [New York: Walter de Gruyter, 1976], p. 154). But see commentary on 49:3.

sion is not only to Israel but also to the Gentiles (cf. 42:1, 6; 49:1, 6–7) it is possible that "weary" has a broader reference, as suggested by H. C. Leupold: "Israelites laboring under the burden of the law and finding no peace, and Gentiles laboring under the oppressive burden of idol-religions that afforded no peace to the burdened conscience of the sinner."[21]

The Servant next explains His preparation by Yahweh to minister to the weary with a sustaining word: "He wakens me morning by morning, wakens my ear to listen like one being taught" (v. 4b). Because Yahweh is the subject of the verbs in this sentence, the discipling process described is actually that of prophetic revelation. Franz J. Delitzsch interprets the phrase "morning by morning" as meaning that the Servant receives revelation after He has awakened, in contrast to those prophets who received visions or dreams by night.[22] Rather, the repetitious term "morning by morning" indicates the daily repetition of the awakening, which is probably not so much physical as spiritual, indicating His receptivity to the message from the Holy Spirit.[23] That is supported by the fact that the "ear," not the eye, is awakened. "The ear with its function of hearing plays a major role in the psychology and anthropology of both O.T. and N.T. It was the organ par excellence whereby man responded to the divine revelation."[24]

Thus the Servant asserts claim to a disciple's ear in preparation for His exercise of a disciple's tongue. There is a direct relationship between the two: the Servant listens to God as a learner, and He speaks to others eloquently, effectively, and encouragingly as a disciple who has learned His lessons well.

The Servant affirms His obedience to the will of Yahweh (v. 5). Verses 5 and 6 both refer to the Servant's submission, but each

---

21. Leupold, *Exposition of Isaiah*, 2:193. Yet from the perspective of fulfillment, Christ's earthly ministry was essentially to Israel (cf. Matt. 10:5–6; 15:24), the Gentile mission being introduced by the apostle Paul in Acts 13.
22. Franz J. Delitzsch, *Isaiah*, Commentary on the Old Testament (Grand Rapids: Eerdmans, 1973), 2:277.
23. See Pieper, *Isaiah II*, p. 390.
24. Muilenburg, "Book of Isaiah," pp. 583–84.

in a different direction. The Servant's voluntary submission to suffering at the hands of men (v. 6) is a result of His willing submission to the plan of Yahweh (v. 5; cf. John 8:28-29). The Servant first testifies positively regarding His obedience to Yahweh's will: "The Sovereign LORD has opened my ears." The phrase "opened my ears" is similar to "wakens my ear" in verse 4. Pieper refers both phrases to the Servant's "inner, moral preparation for learning."[25] Rather, the meaning is simply "to instruct" or "to reveal"[26] (cf. Ruth 4:4; 1 Sam. 9:15). The expression should probably be viewed as a synecdoche of the part for the whole: "ear" represents the whole "body" or "person," given over to knowing and doing God's will (cf. the similar expression in Ps. 40:6-8 as extended to "body" in Heb. 10:5-7).[27]

The Servant's positive statement about receiving divine instruction is followed by a twofold negation: "I have not been rebellious; I have not drawn back." The Servant is characterized neither by an inner attitude of rebellion nor by an outward manifestation of hesitancy. In that regard He is unlike Yahweh's other servant, the nation Israel (cf. Isa. 3:8; 59:4; 63:10; Jer. 4:17; Ezek. 20:13). "Drawing back" can convey the idea of apostasy (Ps. 44:18) or unfaithfulness (Jer. 38:22). Comparison may be made to "a yoke of oxen, who go backward instead of forward, and will not suffer themselves to be guided."[28] In contrast, the Servant willingly received and proclaimed the prophetic word—He was obedient to Yahweh's call and commission. Having an attitude of submission to the word and will of Yahweh, He obediently proclaimed comfort to the weary. But His message

25. Pieper, *Isaiah II*, p. 390; cf. Edward J. Young, *The Book of Isaiah: The English Text, with Introduction, Exposition, and Notes* (Grand Rapids: Eerdmans, 1965-72), 3:299.
26. Hengstenberg, *Christology of the Old Testament*, 2:252.
27. Personal correspondence from Kenneth L. Barker, March 1, 1982. An alternate possibility is to view the figure as a metonymy of cause for effect, the organ of receptivity (the ear) being used for the act of reception.
28. E. W. Hengstenberg, *Christology of the Old Testament and a Commentary on the Messianic Predictions*, abridged ed. (Grand Rapids: Kregel, 1970), p. 227.

also offended the self-righteous, for not all responded positively to His word (v. 6).

The Servant attests His submission to suffering (v. 6). The Servant's testimony turns from His underlying obedience to Yahweh to His outward submission to suffering at the hands of men: "I offered my back to those who beat me, my cheeks to those who pulled out my beard; I did not hide my face from mocking and spitting" (v. 6). The active verbs indicate the Servant's conscious and willing submission to His sufferings. That submission to suffering is indicated in the gospels in such passages as John 10:18: "No one takes it [my life] from me, but I lay it down of my own accord."

Leupold claims that all the forms of ill-treatment mentioned in verse 6 were traditional ways of treating criminals (cf. Num. 12:14; Deut. 25:9; Neh. 13:25; Matt. 26:67; 27:30).[29] "I offered my back to those who beat me" probably denotes in this passage a public punishment, at least a beating or scourging by authorities (cf. Deut. 25:2–3; Jer. 20:2; 37:15).[30] Pulling out the beard was a sign of contempt (Neh. 13:25) as were "mocking and spitting" (Deut. 25:9; Num. 12:14; Job 30:10). Thus we have a startling prophecy of the mistreatment of Christ on the morning of the crucifixion. Although there is no indication in Isaiah 50 that the sufferings culminate in death, the passage prepares the way for the details of Isaiah 53.

THE REJECTED SERVANT EXPRESSES CONFIDENCE THAT
YAHWEH WILL VINDICATE HIM (50:7–9)

Having reported His obedience and sufferings as the committed Disciple of Yahweh, the rejected Servant yet expresses confidence that Yahweh is on His side and will vindicate Him. Thus verses 7–9 take on the form of a confession of trust (cf. Isa. 42:4; 49:4–5).

The Servant asserts His determination because of His confidence

29. Leupold, *Exposition of Isaiah*, 2:194.
30. North, *Second Isaiah*, p. 203; Whybray, who misidentifies the Servant as "Deutero-Isaiah," thinks he has been arrested and put on trial (cf. v. 8) by the Babylonian authorities (*Isaiah 40–66*, p. 151).

in Yahweh's aid (v. 7). The Servant expresses His trust in the vindicating aid of Yahweh: "Because the Sovereign LORD helps me" (v. 7a). Although the verb עָזַר (*'āzar*, "help, support") frequently refers to military assistance either by human armies (Isa. 30:7; 31:3) or by divine intervention (2 Chron. 14:11; 25:8; 26:7), it also refers to personal assistance of a nonmilitary nature (e.g., Ps. 22:11; 107:12; 119:173, 175).[31] It is normally interpreted in this verse as divine enablement of the Servant to endure His sufferings, especially the contempt and scorn of the preceding verse.[32] Pieper suggests that "it is not so much outward, physical support, as spiritual support for His soul; it is preservation in obedience, in patience, in the holy will."[33] However, the expression of confidence in Yahweh's help is asserted again in verse 9 in a legal context, and that may affect the meaning here. The verb may have a legal nuance in both verses, referring to the help of a judge or advocate at court.

In view of Yahweh's expected help, the Servant confidently proclaims, "I will not be disgraced . . . and I know I will not be put to shame" (v. 7b, d). Westermann points out the apparent contradiction between this statement and that in verse 6, "I did not hide my face from mocking" (lit., "shame," from the same root as "disgraced" in v. 7b). Westermann contends:

> This contradiction must not be resolved by making it simply a matter of succession of time—"I take this shame upon me now, but God will take it away from me later." Even if such a succession in time is implied, what is emphasized is that God is to bring the past and present acts of hostility and abuse into constructive connection with the Servant's justification.[34]

However, the fact that the Servant's sufferings culminate in His substitutionary death for sinners (Isa. 53) and are fulfilled in the

31. R. Laird Harris, Gleason L. Archer, Jr., and Bruce K. Waltke, eds., *Theological Wordbook of the Old Testament* (Chicago: Moody, 1980), 2:660–61.
32. E.g., Albert Barnes, "Isaiah," in *Notes on the Old Testament Explanatory and Practical* (reprint, Grand Rapids: Baker, 1979), 2:222.
33. Pieper, *Isaiah II*, 2:392.
34. Westermann, *Isaiah 40–66*, p. 231.

sufferings and death of Jesus Christ requires a more explicit understanding than Westermann has offered of the time factor involved in the Servant's vindication. That matter will be pursued further in the treatment of verses 8–9.

The Servant's confidence in Yahweh's help and implied future vindication give Him fresh strength to endure the sufferings at hand: "Therefore have I set my face like flint" (v. 7c). These words of resolute determination convey "a common description of firmness and determination as expressed in the countenance"[35] (cf. Luke 9:51). Although the expression can describe determination to do evil (cf. Jer. 5:3; Zech. 7:12), it is obvious that obedience to Yahweh's will characterizes the Servant's determination. Leupold suggests that the Servant "will not give his adversaries the satisfaction of seeing him flinch when maltreated."[36]

The Servant challenges His adversaries and anticipates vindication by Yahweh (v. 8). The Servant's defiant challenge to anyone to step forward and participate in a legal contest[37] with Him is prefaced by His confident assertion that Yahweh will vindicate Him. "He who vindicates me is near" (v. 8a). Charged with guilt by His adversaries (thus the punishment rendered in v. 6), the Servant anticipates that in the face of unjust accusations Yahweh will not only conduct His case but will also secure and pronounce His acquittal.[38] It is a question of the guilt or innocence of the suffering Servant. Yahweh, who called, commissioned, and discipled His Servant, will also justify Him, declare Him to be in the right, and vindicate Him.

But when did the vindication occur? Because the Servant's sufferings led to death (Isa. 53:5, 8–10), this would appear to be

35. Alexander, *Commentary*, 2:252.
36. Leupold, *Exposition of Isaiah*, 2:295.
37. Numerous legal terms are in this verse: "to draw near" (cf. Isa. 41:1), "to justify, vindicate" (cf. Deut. 25:1), "to condemn, bring charges" (cf. Deut. 25:1), "to face another" as before the judgment seat (cf. Num. 27:2, 5), "adversary, accuser" (a hapax legomenon, but cf. Ex. 24:14).
38. North, *Second Isaiah*, p. 204. Westermann (*Isaiah 40–66*, p. 231) holds the unusual view that the Servant has already conceded His defeat by submitting to punishment, so that in the adversaries' eyes the case is already decided and the Servant has lost.

a sort of postmortem inquest (cf. Isa. 53:11). Henri Blocher thus speaks of His "acquittal by resurrection."[39] (Ps. 22 supports that view, with the resurrection of Messiah understood as occurring between vv. 21 and 22.) Hengstenberg says, "It took place and was fulfilled, in the first instance, in the resurrection and glorification of Christ, and, then in the destruction of Jerusalem"[40] (cf. 1 Tim. 3:16). Any fulfillment in the destruction of Jerusalem in A.D. 70 is dubious, except as that event may anticipate the attack on the city near the end of the future Great Tribulation followed by the return of Yahweh's Servant to establish the messianic kingdom.

Thus, in terms of fuller New Testament revelation, the vindication of the Servant takes place in two stages: (1) the threefold exaltation described in Isaiah 52:13 (fulfilled in the resurrection, ascension, and present session of Jesus Christ); and (2) the final enthronement of the Servant over the millennial kingdom following His second advent. Both stages of that vindication demonstrate the error in the Servant's adversaries' view that He was deserted by God as punishment for His own sin (Isa. 53:4b; cf. Ps. 22:7–8).

In view of His certain vindication by Yahweh (the Servant is innocent!), He challenges His adversaries: "Who then will bring charges against me? Let us face each other! Who is my accuser? Let him confront me!" (v. 8b). The term "accuser" (lit. "owner of my case") is found only here in the Old Testament and refers to "the one who possesses a judgment against him."[41]

The Servant expects the defeat of His adversaries (v. 9). The Servant summarizes and restates His confidence in and vindication by Yahweh (as already referred to in vv. 7–8): "It is the Sovereign LORD who helps me. Who is he that will condemn me?" (v. 9a). Yahweh, the sovereign Creator of the universe, is the One who helps the Servant as advocate or judge; who can possibly win a verdict against Him? The rhetorical question calls for only one answer, and the negative reply is amplified in a

39. Blocher, *Songs of the Servant*, p. 50.
40. Hengstenberg, *Christology of the Old Testament*, 2:254.
41. Young, *Book of Isaiah*, 3:302.

description of the would-be adversaries by a simile ("they will all wear out like a garment") and a metaphor ("the moths will eat them up," v. 9*b*), "common images of gradual but inevitable destruction."[42] Pieper suggests that "the picture is not to be understood as referring to physical disintegration (although that too would not be out of place); but the meaning is that the accusations of the enemies will collapse before the righteous judgment of the Lord and be put to shame like the moldering of a moth-eaten garment.[43]

In summary of the first two strophes of this song, four features stand out regarding the Servant: (1) the Servant is a righteous Sufferer (vv. 4–5); (2) the Servant is a voluntary Sufferer (v. 6); (3) the Servant has learned submission from Yahweh (vv. 4–5); and (4) the Servant retains confidence in Yahweh despite suffering (v. 9).[44]

YAHWEH CONTRASTS THE OBEDIENT WALK OF THE SERVANT'S DISCIPLES WITH THE JUDGMENT TO COME ON THE WICKED (50:10–11)

[10]Who among you fears the LORD
      and obeys the word of his servant?
Let him who walks in the dark,
      who has no light,
trust in the name of the LORD
      and rely on his God.
[11]But now, all you who light fires
      and provide yourselves with flaming torches,
go, walk in the light of your fires
      and of the torches you have set ablaze.
This is what you shall receive from my hand:
      You will lie down in torment.

42. Skinner, *Book of the Prophet*, p. 115.
43. Pieper, *Isaiah II*, p. 394.
44. Mark A. Arrington, "The Identification of the Anonymous Servant in Isaiah 40–55" (Th.M. thesis, Dallas Theological Seminary, 1971), pp. 40–44.

This difficult unit is composed of an exhortation (v. 10) and
a warning or threat (v. 11). The judgment aspect of this unit is
related to the preceding verses: "The judgment against the faith-
less needs the portrayal of the servant as a faithful disciple who
teaches God's word."[45]

Difference of opinion exists as to the speaker's identity in
these verses. One view regards the Servant as still speaking
throughout verses 10-11.[46] Ivan Engnell agrees, except that he
attributes the final line of verse 11 ("This is what you shall
receive . . . ") to Yahweh.[47] R. N. Whybray regards the servant
(whom he sees as the prophet) as speaking in verse 10, with
Yahweh speaking in verse 11.[48] However, others correctly view
Yahweh as the speaker throughout verses 10-11. James Muilenburg thus affirms that "the speaker throughout is Yahweh; the
shifts from third to first person are characteristic of prophetic
style."[49]

The content of Yahweh's speech thus draws a contrast between the righteous and the wicked: (1) Yahweh exhorts the
Servant's disciples to walk by faith in the darkness (v. 10), and
(2) Yahweh warns the unfaithful that their self-centered efforts
will result in judgment (v. 11).

YAHWEH EXHORTS THE SERVANT'S DISCIPLES TO WALK BY FAITH
IN THE DARKNESS (50:10)

A major problem in this verse is the grammatical structure.
Is the opening pronoun in the Hebrew text (מִי, mî) interrogative
("Who?") or indefinite ("Whoever")?[50] If interrogative, how far
does the question extend (i.e., are the second and third lines

45. Melugin, *Formation of Isaiah*, p. 73.
46. Hengstenberg, *Christology of the Old Testament*, 2:254; MacRae, *Gospel of Isaiah*, p. 119.
47. Engnell, "'Ebed Yahweh Songs," p. 71. Engnell identifies the speech in verses 10-11b as "in the typical royal third person style."
48. Whybray, *Isaiah 40–66*, p. 153.
49. Muilenburg, "Book of Isaiah," p. 587.
50. Pieper regards the pronoun as indefinite, introductory to noun clauses in the first and second lines, with the third line constituting an independent clause ("Let him trust . . . ") (*Isaiah II*, p. 394). Cf. Young, *Book of Isaiah*, 3:303, and cf. the translation in the *Jerusalem Bible*.

subordinate or independent)? English versions have placed the question mark at the end of different lines in the verse. The *Revised Standard Version* continues the question to the end of the verse, subordinating the second and third lines as descriptions of the "servant, who walks in darkness and has not light, yet trusts in the name of the LORD. . . . " The King James Version places the question mark after the second line, thus subordinating the second line to "you," and making the third line independent ("Who is among you that feareth the Lord, that obeyeth the voice of his servant, that walketh in darkness, and hath no light? let him trust . . . ").[51] Those translations (such as the NIV) that place the question mark at the end of the first line and translate the remaining independent clauses as exhortations give the smoothest sense to the passage.[52]

Consequently the addressees in verse 10 ("Who among you . . . ") are the faithful in contrast to the unfaithful "you" of verse 11. Yahweh inquires concerning the identity of the faithful who are obedient to the word proclaimed by Yahweh's suffering but vindicated Servant: "Who among you fears the LORD and obeys the word of his servant?" (v. 10a). Reverential awe of Yahweh and obedience to His Servant's word are complementary. As Pieper states, "He who honors and fears the Lord, honors His Messenger also, John 5:23. The proof of the fear of the Lord lies in giving ear to the word and voice of the Servant, and yielding obedience to Him, for the Servant's word is God's Word."[53]

Yahweh's exhortation to those who walk by faith and not by sight ("who walks in the dark, who has no light" [v. 10b]) is clear: "Let him . . . trust in the name of the LORD and rely on his God" (v. 10c). This is an exhortation to the righteous to do what the Servant has done, to be His faithful disciples. Thus "the verse is an admirable summary, and application, of vv. 4-9."[54]

51. Cf. Leupold, *Exposition of Isaiah*, 2:196-97.
52. The *New English Bible* places the question mark after the first line but regards the rest of the verse as the answer to the question.
53. Pieper, *Isaiah II*, p. 395.
54. North, *Second Isaiah*, p. 205.

YAHWEH WARNS THE UNFAITHFUL THAT THEIR SELF-CENTERED
EFFORTS WILL RESULT IN JUDGMENT (50:11)

The movement from exhorting the faithful to rebuking satirically the unfaithful is clear in this verse. But "the metaphors are
no longer clear to us."[55] The judgment pronounced at the end of
the verse makes it transparent that the ungodly are addressed.
They are described as "all you who light fires and provide your-
selves with flaming torches" (v. 11a) and are exhorted, apparently satirically, to "go, walk in the light of your fires and of the
torches you have set ablaze" (v. 11b).

The reference may be to the self-righteous schemes of the
ungodly who seek to provide their own light for the path of life
rather than trusting Yahweh to provide light in the darkness
(v. 10). Thus Albert Barnes comments:

> The idea probably is, that all human devices for salvation bear the
> same resemblance to the true plan proposed by God, which a
> momentary spark in the dark does to the clear shining of a bright
> light like that of the sun. If this is the sense, it is a most graphic
> and striking description of the nature of all the schemes by which
> the sinner hopes to save himself.[56]

An alternate interpretation of the figure is that the wicked
somehow fall into the trap that they have set for the righteous;
the destruction they intended for the Servant and His disciples is
turned back on them by Yahweh.[57] In any event they are marked
out by Yahweh for judgment on their schemes: "This is what you
shall receive from my hand: You will lie down in torment"
(v. 11b). Christopher R. North understands this last phrase as
"'a place of (fiery) torment,' very nearly 'Gehenna.'"[58]

Hengstenberg sets the contrast of the two verses in vivid
metaphor: "The pious walk patiently through the darkness, until

55. D. F. Payne, "Isaiah," in The New Layman's Bible Commentary, ed.
    G. C. D. Howley, F. F. Bruce, and H. L. Ellison (Grand Rapids: Zonder-
    van, 1979), p. 806.
56. Barnes, "Isaiah," 2:225.
57. Cf. Whybray, Isaiah 40–66, p. 154; Delitzsch, Isaiah, 2:280–81.
58. North, Second Isaiah, p. 206.

Jehovah kindles a light for them. The ungodly kindle a fire *for themselves*; but the fire, that should light and warm, consumes them."[59]

CONCLUSION

The committed Servant-Disciple of Yahweh reports not only His past submission to the plan of Yahweh but also His voluntary sufferings at the hands of men, and implies that by His rejection He has learned to comfort the weary. In the wake of that rejection, He expresses confidence that Yahweh, who has discipled Him, will also vindicate Him. Consequently Yahweh exhorts the Servant's disciples (following the Servant's example) to walk by faith in darkness but threatens the unfaithful that their self-righteous efforts will end in judgment. The fulfillment of this prophecy is found in the sufferings and exaltation of Jesus Christ and in the response of the righteous and the wicked to Him.

59. Hengstenberg, *Christology of the Old Testament*, abridged ed., p. 229.

5

The Career of the Servant
Isaiah 52:13—53:12

The fourth Servant song (Isa. 52:13—53:12) "may without
any exaggeration be called the most important text of the Old
Testament."[1] That is demonstrated first by its numerous citations
in the New Testament (e.g., Luke 22:37; Acts 8:30–35; 1 Pet.
2:22–25)[2] and second by the voluminous Jewish and Christian

1. Ivan Engnell, "The 'Ebed Yahweh Songs and the Suffering Messiah in
   Deutero-Isaiah," *Bulletin of John Rylands Library* 31 (January 1948):73.
   Delitzsch has called this prophecy "the most central, the deepest, and the
   loftiest thing that the Old Testament prophecy, outstripping itself, has ever
   achieved" (Franz J. Delitzsch, *Isaiah*, Commentary on the Old Testament
   [Grand Rapids: Eerdmans, 1973], 2:203.
2. If lost from the Old Testament, this passage could almost be reconstructed
   from its quotations in the New Testament (Page H. Kelley, "Isaiah," in *The
   Broadman Bible Commentary*, ed. C. J. Allen [Nashville: Broadman, 1971],
   5:340–41). Culver has observed, "Perhaps the most distinguished thing
   about it [Isa. 52:13—53:12] is the fact that this very portion stands in the
   background of almost every New Testament treatment of the great events
   connected with our Lord's passion, death, burial, resurrection, ascension,
   exaltation, and second coming" (Robert D. Culver, *The Sufferings and the
   Glory of the Lord's Righteous Servant* [Moline, Ill.: Christian Service Foundation, 1958], p. 20).

literature that has been based on this prophecy down through the centuries.[3]

The messianic significance of the song is the basis of the New Testament quotations and accounts in large part for the extensive debate that surrounds it. Although the sufferings of Christ are described at length in the song (says F. B. Meyer, "There is only one brow which this crown of thorns will fit"[4]), the dominant theme in reality is the exaltation of Christ "*victorious and triumphant* through his vicarious sufferings."[5] August Pieper perceives that the theme of the prophecy is "not the suffering of the Servant as such, but rather His triumph over suffering and His exaltation out of this humiliation."[6] Page H. Kelley similarly points out that the song is not primarily concerned with suffering, for the suffering has already come to an end: it is described in the past tense in 53:3–6, and the verbs in the future tense speak of the Servant's triumph and glory—52:12; 53:10–11.[7] (It is noteworthy that only a premillennial understanding of Christ's second advent recognizes the fullest significance of the Servant's exaltation.[8])

The twofold theme of "the sufferings of Christ and the glories that would follow" (1 Pet. 1:11) draws together the prominent thematic threads of the preceding Servant songs. As the first two songs (Isa. 42:1–9; 49:1–13) emphasized the ultimate success of Yahweh's Servant-Messiah while alluding to His sufferings (42:4; 49:4), so the third song (50:4–11) emphasized the sufferings and patient endurance of the Servant while implying His ultimate vindication or exaltation (50:7–9). The distinctive

3. "The extant literature on the monumental fifty-third chapter of Isaiah is so vast that, perhaps, no person could read it in a lifetime" (Robert F. Pfeiffer, p. 3 of preface to Frederick Alfred Aston, *The Challenge of the Ages: New Light on Isaiah 53*, rev. ed. [Scarsdale, N.Y.: Research, 1969]).

4. F. B. Meyer, *Christ in Isaiah: Expositions of Isaiah XL–LV* (New York: Revell, 1895), p. 158; for the identification of the Servant of Yahweh with the Davidic Messiah, see chapter 6.

5. Engnell, "'Ebed Yahweh Songs," p. 74.

6. August Pieper, *Isaiah II: An Exposition of Isaiah 40–66* (1919; trans., Milwaukee: Northwestern, 1979), pp. 430–31.

7. Kelley, "Isaiah," 5:341.

8. Merrill F. Unger, *Unger's Commentary on the Old Testament* (Chicago: Moody, 1981), 2:1293–1301.

contribution of the fourth song is to present the details and purpose of the Servant's sufferings and death, particularly as they relate to His exaltation and the ultimate success of His mission.

Unlike scholarly opinion on the other Servant songs, there is a general agreement on the extent of the fourth song: 52:13–15 constitutes an introduction or prologue to 53:1–12. R. N. Whybray's dissenting opinion that 52:13–15 is a separate and unrelated poem is based on his unwarranted view that chapter 53 is "a song of thanksgiving for the deliverance of God's servant, Deutero-Isaiah, from mortal danger."[9] But scholars disagree on nearly everything else concerning the passage. Problems abound regarding the text, translation, and interpretation of virtually every verse in the song. However, evangelical scholars have given unanimous assent that the Servant in the passage is the Lord Jesus Christ.

As in the preceding two Servant songs, the fourth song also begins a cycle of thought that culminates in a powerful message of salvation in 54:1–17.[10]

One major problem is the identification of the speakers. It is clear that Yahweh is speaking in 52:13–15 and again in 53:10 or 11–12. The intervening verses (53:1–9 or 10) are a report about the humiliation, sufferings, and sacrificial death of the Servant. Thus the song is a report within a divine utterance, beginning and ending with Yahweh speaking. But who are the speakers of the report? Three groups have generally been suggested: (1) the prophet Isaiah (some say "Deutero-Isaiah") as representative of a group (usually the prophets);[11] (2) the Gentile

9. R. N. Whybray, *Isaiah 40–66* (Grand Rapids: Eerdmans, 1981), p. 169; cf. R. N. Whybray, *Thanksgiving for a Liberated Prophet: An Interpretation of Isaiah Chapter 53* (Sheffield: Journal For the Study of the Old Testament, 1978); see also H. M. Orlinsky, "The So-Called 'Suffering Servant' in Isaiah 53," in *Interpreting the Prophetic Tradition*, ed. H. M. Orlinsky (New York: Hebrew Union College, 1969), pp. 229–32.
10. Cf. Robert B. Chisolm, "Toward a Form Critical/Structural Analysis of Isaiah" (student paper, Dallas Theological Seminary, 1980), pp. 62–63.
11. E.g., E. W. Hengstenberg, *Christology of the Old Testament and a Commentary on the Messianic Predictions*, abridged ed. (Grand Rapids: Kregel, 1970), p. 234.

kings of 52:15;[12] or (3) the believing Jewish remnant.[13] I will
present evidence for the third view. Because no addressees are
indicated in the text, it is probably best to assume that both the
divine utterance and the report of the believing remnant are
addressed potentially to all mankind, as with the first Servant
song (42:1–4).

The message of 52:13—53:12 thus materializes: Yahweh
announces the exaltation of His Servant because of His satisfactory substitutionary death for the sins of both His guilty people
and the Gentiles. The passage consists of five strophes, the central
three of which compose the body of the report. Thus the message
has three units: (1) an introductory appraisal in which Yahweh
promises to supremely exalt His Servant, who though deeply
degraded will both purify and receive the worship of nations
(52:13–15); (2) a confessional report in which believing Israelites
contrast their past rejection of the Servant with the true meaning
of His death (53:1–9); and (3) a concluding epilogue in which
Yahweh promises to exalt His Servant because He did His will in
dying as a guilt offering (53:10–12).

Yahweh Announces the Exaltation of His Servant Who Has Become Deeply Degraded to Purify Many Nations (52:13–15)

[13]See, my servant will act wisely;
    he will be raised and lifted up and highly exalted.
[14]Just as there were many who were apalled at him—
    his appearance was so disfigured beyond that of any man
    and his form marred beyond human likeness—
[15]so will he sprinkle many nations,
    and kings will shut their mouths because of him.
  For what they were not told, they will see,
    and what they have not heard, they will understand.

---

12. E.g., James Muilenburg, "The Book of Isaiah: Chapters 40–66," in *The Interpreter's Bible*, ed. George A. Buttrick (Nashville: Abingdon, 1956), 5:614.
13. E.g., Delitzsch, *Isaiah*, 2:310–11.

Yahweh's announcement of His Servant's exaltation (v. 13) is developed along two lines: initially, many were appalled at Him who was humbled below what was human (v. 14; cf. 53:1-9); but ultimately kings and nations who have experienced His provision of purification from sins are amazed that He is exalted above what is human (v. 15; cf. 53:10-12).[14] Gerhard von Rad has aptly observed, "The unusual aspect of this great poem is that it begins with what is really the end of the whole story, the Servant's glorification and the recognition of his significance for the world."[15] In part, these verses contain the vindication anticipated by the Servant in 50:8-9.[16] Thus in this divine utterance Yahweh (1) announces that His Servant will achieve success (52:13) and (2) compares initial Jewish consternation with ultimate Gentile comprehension (vv. 14-15).

YAHWEH ANNOUNCES THAT HIS SERVANT
WILL ACHIEVE SUCCESS (52:13)

The Servant's success will come through wise action (v. 13a). Before describing the exaltation of the Servant, Yahweh affirms that it is the Servant's wise and effective action that will achieve success: "See, my servant will act wisely." Allan A. MacRae correctly observes that this affirmation is a "general statement of the effective accomplishment of the great work of the Servant."[17]

Through the use of the demonstrative particle הִנֵּה (*hinnēh*, "see"), Yahweh both points to the Servant as if He were present (confirmed by the direct address to the Servant in v. 14) and calls attention to the person and theme now to be introduced,[18]

---

14. Cf. Claus Westermann, *Isaiah 40-66: A Commentary* (Philadelphia: Westminster, 1975), p. 255.

15. Gerhard von Rad, *The Message of the Prophets* (New York: Harper & Row, 1968), p. 223.

16. See commentary on 50:8-9 in chapter 4.

17. Allan A. MacRae, *The Gospel of Isaiah* (Chicago: Moody, 1977), p. 131. Delitzsch has noted, "This very first verse contains, according to Isaiah's custom, a brief, condensed explanation of the theme" (*Isaiah*, 2:304).

18. W. Urwick, *The Servant of Jehovah: A Commentary, Grammatical and Critical, Upon Isaiah LII. 13—LIII. 12* (Edinburgh: T. & T. Clark, 1877), p. 98.

102   The Servant Songs

a theme that is "startlingly new and wonderfully important."[19]
Claus Westermann correctly recognizes the deliberate identification between the opening words in this verse ("See, my servant")
and the opening words of the first Servant song (in 42:1 the NIV
translates this same Hebrew phrase as "Here is my servant"). He
indicates that "the two songs go together in that 42:1–4 show
the origin of the Servant's work—his designation to his office by
God—and chs. 52f. its culmination—God proclaims the success
of his servant's way and work."[20]

Yahweh's Servant is named again in this prophecy only in
53:11. He speaks nowhere in the song and, except for the "you"
(NIV footnote) in 52:14, He is spoken of in the third person
throughout. George Adam Smith indicates that "we never hear
or see Himself. But all the more solemnly is He there: a shadow
upon countless faces, a grievous memory on the hearts of the
speakers."[21]

The *New International Version* translates the Hebrew word
יַשְׂכִּיל (*yaśkîl*) as "will act wisely" in the text and "will prosper"
in a footnote.[22] Both ideas are contained in the Hebrew word,
which has the primary meaning of either "to possess wisdom"
(i.e., "be wise," e.g., Ps. 2:10) or "to use wisdom" (i.e., "act
wisely," e.g., 1 Sam. 18:5) or a secondary sense of "to be pros-
perous or successful" (e.g., Josh. 1:7–8; 2 Kings 18:7; Prov. 17:8;
Jer. 10:21).[23] Franz J. Delitzsch points out that "the word is never
applied to such prosperity as a man enjoys without any effort on
his own, but only to such as he attains by successful action."[24]

A decision as to the correct nuance of *yaśkîl* in this verse

19. Culver, *The Sufferings and the Glory*, p. 23.
20. Westermann, *Isaiah 40–66*, p. 258.
21. George Adam Smith, *The Book of Isaiah*, 2 vols., The Expositor's Bible
    (New York: Hodder & Stroughton, n.d.), 2:342.
22. G. R. Driver's revocalization of the verb to read יְשֻׂכַּל (*yiśśākēl*, "he will
    be bound," that is, "bound as a form of punishment, such as hanging")
    is unwarranted ("Isaiah 52:13—53:12: The Servant of the Lord," in
    Matthew Black and Georg Fohrer, eds., *In Memorium Paul Kahle* [Berlin:
    Alfred Töpelmann, 1968], p. 90).
23. Urwick sees this secondary meaning growing out of a metonymy of effect
    for cause, the resultant process being indicated for the wisdom itself
    (*Servant of Jehovah*, p. 98).
24. Delitzsch, *Isaiah*, 2:305.

depends in part on one's understanding of the relationship between the two clauses in the verse. Is the exaltation described in verse 13b the result of the verb, which would then be translated "will act wisely," or is the exaltation a parallel description with the verb, which would then be translated "will prosper or be successful"? If the former meaning were correct, the word would probably identify the Servant's effective action in dying as a substitutionary sacrifice for sin, that being the only pathway to ultimate success and exaltation. With that meaning in mind, Robert D. Culver states, "However tragic the event appeared to be, the most practical, profitable, and successful event in the history of the world was the death of Christ."[25] Culver's statement is of course true, and the general idea of this interpretation does fit into the context. However, in view of the ambiguity of yaśkîl in this verse, the preference for recognizing synonymous parallelism between the two lines assumes priority and indicates that the translation "will prosper," that is, by being exalted, is the preferable one.[26] Some scholars seek to combine both ideas in the meaning of the verb,[27] and the choice of views and translations does not greatly affect the overall thought of the verse.

The Servant's success is described as exaltation (v. 13b). The success that Yahweh has announced for His Servant is described in terms of highest exaltation: "he will be raised and lifted up and highly exalted." The success of the Servant is unfolded in three verbs that presuppose the inhuman degradation that is viewed in verse 14. This clause does not describe the result or consequences of the verb yaśkîl in the preceding clause[28] (although it does describe the results of the implied wise and effective action that led to the success indicated in that verb). Yahweh draws on three verbs of exaltation (the first two of which

25. Culver, *The Sufferings and the Glory*, p. 28; cf. Smith, *Book of Isaiah*, 2:347; Joseph A. Alexander, *Commentary on the Prophecies of Isaiah* (Grand Rapids: Zondervan, 1953), 2:226.

26. Cf. MacRae, *Gospel of Isaiah*, p. 131.

27. Whybray, *Isaiah 40–66*, p. 169; Westermann, *Isaiah 40–66*, p. 258.

28. Contra Delitzsch, *Isaiah*, 2:305; MacRae, *Gospel of Isaiah*, p. 131; Edward J. Young, *The Book of Isaiah: The English Text, with Introduction, Exposition, and Notes* (Grand Rapids: Eerdmans, 1965–72), 3:335; also see note 25 above.

are reminiscent of Yahweh's own exaltation in Isa. 6:1; cf. 57:15)
to describe the Servant's "superlative degree of success."[29] Are
these verbs synonymous or sequential? W. Urwick is an example
of those scholars who view these terms as an "accumulation of
synonyms"[30] used to exhibit the glorious exaltation of the Servant "to the height of God Himself."[31] Others regard the verbs
as describing "the commencement, the continuation, and the
result or climax of the exaltation."[32] Pieper specifies that they
"precisely foretold the resurrection . . . the ascension into
heaven . . . and the sitting at the right hand of the Father."[33] In
general, the passage finds fulfillment in the postresurrection exaltation of Christ (cf. Acts 2:33; 5:31; Phil. 2:9) and, retrospec-
tively, appropriately allows for the three stages in that exaltation.

YAHWEH COMPARES INITIAL JEWISH CONSTERNATION AT THE SERVANT
WITH ULTIMATE GENTILE COMPREHENSION (52:14–15)

A comparison is introduced in verse 14 with the words
"Just as" (the Hebrew comparative conjunction is כַּאֲשֶׁר,
ka'ʾasher). A problem of syntax and interpretation arises in identifying the apodosis (the "even so" clause) that completes the
comparison begun in the protasis, "Just as there were many who
were appalled at him" (v. 14a). The problem is due in part to
the presence of two clauses beginning with "so" (כֵּן, kēn), either
of which may complete the comparison (vv. 14b and 15a). At
least three solutions have been suggested:[34] (1) Several scholars
have suggested that the protasis (v. 14a) is followed by a double
apodosis (vv. 14b, 15a).[35] (2) Edward J. Young has claimed that

29. H. C. Leupold, *Exposition of Isaiah* (Grand Rapids: Baker, 1971), 2:224.
30. Urwick, *Servant of Jehovah*, p. 99.
31. Gleason L. Archer, "Isaiah," in *The Wycliffe Bible Commentary*, ed.
    Charles F. Pfeiffer and Everett F. Harrison (Chicago: Moody, 1962),
    p. 646.
32. Delitzsch, *Isaiah*, 2:305.
33. Pieper, *Isaiah II*, p. 431.
34. Cf. Robert R. Dewbury, "An Exegetical Study of Isaiah 52:13—53:12,"
    (Th.M. thesis, Dallas Theological Seminary, 1975), p. 25.
35. "As thus explained, the sense would be, their abhorrence of him was not
    without reason ('so marred from man his look . . .'), and it shall not be
    without requital ('so shall he sprinkle many nations')" (Alexander, *Com-
    mentary*, 2:287); cf. W. H. Brownlee, *The Meaning of the Qumran Scrolls
    for the Bible* (New York: Oxford U., 1964), p. 292.

both *kēn* clauses are to be understood parenthetically, with the apodosis suggested in the second clause of verse 15 ("and kings will shut their mouths because of him").[36] However, (3) the majority of scholars correctly view verse 14b as an explanatory parenthesis and verse 15a (actually the first two cola of the Hebrew text) as the completion of the comparison.[37] More specifically, although the apodosis does begin with the first colon of verse 15 ("so will he sprinkle many nations"), the structural points of the comparison with verse 14a are found in the second colon ("and kings will shut their mouths because of him"). "Just as many were appalled at his inhuman treatment and disfigurement and death, so 'kings' will be astonished when they comprehend the meaning of His debasement and the universal application of that death."[38] Thus the comparison is between the "many" individuals (mainly Israelites) who are appalled at the fact of the Servant's suffering, and the "kings" (representative of "many" nations) who will be awed at the effects (expiatory purification or cleansing) that will result from the Servant's suffering.

Many were appalled at the Servant's inhuman disfigurement (v. 14). As already indicated, this verse begins with the protasis of a comparison: "Just as there were many who were appalled at him" (v. 14a). The "many" individuals who are "appalled at him" are probably Israelites, in contrast to the "many nations,

---

36. Young, *Book of Isaiah*, 3:336–37. "Thus the contrast appears between the action of the many with respect to the servant and that of the kings; the many are astounded, the kings close their mouths" (p. 337).
37. E.g., Delitzsch, *Isaiah*, 2:306; Leupold, *Exposition of Isaiah*, 2:224; Westermann, *Isaiah 40–66*, p. 258; Unger, *Commentary*, 2:1294–95.
38. Kenneth L. Barker, personal correspondence, April 14, 1982. Barker has recognized this structural correspondence in the comparison: עָלָיו (*'ālāyw*, v. 15) answers to עָלֶיךָ (*'āleykā*, v. 14), יִקְפְּצוּ (*yiqp'sû*, v. 15) answers to שָׁמְמוּ (*shām'mû*, v. 14), מְלָכִים (*m'lākîm*, v. 15) answers to רַבִּים (*rabbîm*, v. 14). Cf. Unger, *Commentary*, 2:1295; Dewbury, "Exegetical Study," p. 26. But many commentators view the comparison in a much more general sense: "The point of the comparison is this: As astonishing as would be his humiliation, so astonishing would be his exaltation (as described in v. 15)" (Archer, "Isaiah," p. 646). Statements of the comparison are affected, of course, by the scholar's view of the verb *yazzeh* in verse 15.

and kings" of verse 15. The term "appalled" is used in Ezekiel 27:35 to describe men's reaction to the ruined city of Tyre. It could be translated "amazed, shocked, aghast, or horrified," and indicates that those who gaze on the Servant are petrified by paralyzing astonishment and stupefying surprise at His deep abasement and degradation. The word is frequently used to describe the reaction to divine judgment (Lev. 26:32; Jer. 18:16; 19:8); so it may also here imply that they think He is suffering for His own sins (as in 53:3-4). The object of the verb in the Hebrew is in the second person: "appalled at you" (NIV footnote). The textual reading "him" is supported only by two Hebrew manuscripts, the Targum, and the Syriac translation, but is adopted by many scholars as more fitting to the context. G. R. Driver retains "you" but with the implied antecedent "my people" (i.e., Israel).[39] It is better with many other scholars to translate "you" with reference to the Servant, for a sudden change in person (cf. the third person in the rest of the verse) is common in Isaiah (cf. 31:6; 42:20).[40] Yahweh has already spoken directly to the Servant in 42:6-7 and 49:8, so it is not unusual here.

The next two lines give a parenthetical reason for the horrified shock at the Servant: "his appearance was so disfigured beyond that of any man and his form marred beyond human likeness" (v. 14b, c). Some scholars think these lines belong after 53:2,[41] but there is no textual support for such a change. The terms "appearance" and "form" clearly refer to the physical appearance of the Servant. Unger understands "appearance" as a "special reference to His face" and "form" as a reference to His "physical body in general."[42] Because that appearance is de-

---

39. Driver, "Isaiah 52:13—53:12," p. 91; in his translation, on the basis of the Targum and rhythm he even inserts after "you" the words "O my people, for many days"! MacRae also takes "you" as Israel scattered in Exile, to which the Servant's appearance is compared in the next line ("the suffering of Israel will be paralleled by the suffering that the Servant must undergo") (Gospel of Isaiah, p. 132). Unfortunately, the New American Standard Bible adopts that rendering.
40. For example, Urwick, Servant of Jehovah, p. 100.
41. Whybray, Isaiah 40–66, p. 169.
42. Unger, Commentary, 2:1294.

scribed in the context of His suffering and death (already implied in 49:4, 7; 50:6), it is not a reference to His normal appearance throughout life. Although Scripture gives no physical description of Christ, it is extremely unlikely that He was repulsive in appearance, as indicated in Christian art before Constantine.[43] Although later Christian art may have idealized His physical attractiveness, the disfigurement described in this verse is the result of His trial-and-death sufferings. "Disfigured"[44] and "marred" describe the results of the Servant's physical suffering, particularly leading up to and including the crucifixion. The extent of His disfigurement is described by the adverbial phrases "beyond that of any man" and "beyond human likeness." Both phrases are introduced by מִן (min), denoting here "away from," that is, destroying all likeness to man, so as to suggest that His appearance no longer appeared human: "He looked like a creature not of our race, so much had sorrow smitten him."[45]

Nations will be purified and kings astonished because of the results of the Servant's disfigurement (v. 15). Just as many individuals were shocked at the Servant's extreme degradation, even so many nations will be purified through His expiatory sufferings, leading to amazement on the part of kings who comprehend all this. The first colon of this compound apodosis ("so will he sprinkle many nations," v. 15a), is one of the most controversial clauses in the fourth Servant song. The contention centers on the meaning of the Hebrew word יַזֶּה (yazzeh, "he will sprinkle"), traditionally understood to be from the verb נָזָה (nāzâ, "to sprinkle"). It is a technical Mosaic word for the sprinkling of water, oil, or blood as a cleansing or purifying ceremony. A. R. Fausset has recognized that nāzâ "universally in the Old Testament means either to sprinkle (with blood); to atone for guilt—as

43. Delitzsch, Isaiah, 2:307.
44. The Hebrew word translated "disfigured" is מִשְׁחַת (mishḥāt), which is represented in the Dead Sea Scroll 1QIsᵃ as משחתי. It has been translated, "I have anointed" (māshaḥtî). As Payne points out, that "would offer something approaching a Messianic identification of the Servant" (David F. Payne, "The Servant of the Lord: Language and Interpretation," The Evangelical Quarterly 43 [July-September 1971]:133).
45. Culver, The Sufferings and the Glory, p. 35.

the high priest makes an *expiation* [Lev. 4:6; 16:14, 19]; or to *sprinkle (with water)*, as synonymous with *purifying* [Num. 19:18, 21] or *cleansing* [cf. Ezek. 36:25, where a different Hebrew word for sprinkle means 'to cleanse']. . . . Both *atoning* for guilt and *purifying* by the Spirit are appropriate to Messiah [John 13:8; Heb. 9:13–14; 10:22; 12:24; 1 Pet. 1:2]."[46]

However, during the past century (since Gesenius) probably the majority of scholars[47] have taken the verb to mean "startle," either by emending the text or by assuming that the verb comes from an otherwise unattested Hebrew root meaning "to startle," which is cognate to an Arabic word meaning "to spring up, jump, leap," as in amazement.[48] Thus the translation proposed by this viewpoint is "many nations will marvel at him" (NIV footnote). That provides a very fitting apodosis for the comparison begun in verse 14*a*. However, Young has championed the meaning "sprinkle,"[49] along with a number of other contemporary scholars.[50] Young has carefully refuted the translation "to

---

46. A. R. Fausset, "Job—Isaiah," in *A Commentary, Critical, Experimental, and Practical on the Old and New Testaments*, by Robert Jamieson, A. R. Fausset, and David Brown (reprint, Grand Rapids: Eerdmans, 1978), 2:728.

47. A. B. Davidson asserted flatly, "It is simple treason against the Hebrew language to render 'sprinkle.' The interpreter who will do so will 'do anything'" (cited by Culver, *The Sufferings and the Glory*, p. 31). Less bluntly but just as assuredly, Pieper states that "there is today [1919] virtually only one opinion" (*Isaiah II*, p. 432). See also Driver, "Isaiah 52:13—53:12," p. 92.

48. Delitzsch, *Isaiah*, 2:308. This view finds support in the LXX, where θαυμάσονται (*thaumasontai*) means "shall wonder" or "be astonished" (cf. Christopher R. North, *The Suffering Servant in Deutero-Isaiah: An Historical and Critical Study*, 2d ed. (London: Oxford U., 1956), p. 123; Urwick, *Servant of Jehovah*, p. 103).

49. Edward J. Young, "The Interpretation of יזה in Isaiah 52:15," *Westminster Theological Journal* (May—October 1941):125–32; reprinted in Edward J. Young, *Studies in Isaiah* (Grand Rapids: Eerdmans, 1954), pp. 199–206. Cf. Young, *Book of Isaiah* 3:338, and the extensive refutation of "startle" in Urwick, *Servant of Jehovah*, pp. 103–4.

50. For example, Unger, *Commentary,*, 2:1295, and von Rad, *The Message of the Prophets*, p. 221; North takes the term in the sense of sprinkling, but for the purpose of neutralizing infection or contagion by the person or thing sprinkled (*The Second Isaiah: Introduction, Translation, and Commentary to Chapters XL—LV* [Oxford: Clarendon, 1964], p. 235).

spring up, to startle" and has satisfactorily answered objections raised against the translation "to sprinkle."[51]

Perhaps the major objection to "sprinkle" is that when so translated, the fluid sprinkled takes the accusative case; and here the "many nations" are in the accusative.[52] However, W. Kay's objection to that argument is still valid: the argument forgets that "in the passage before us the verb refers, not to a literal process of *sprinkling*, but to an act of purification *analogous* to that which was effected by ceremonial sprinkling."[53] Another objection, that a priestly role is out of context for the Servant in this passage, has been countered by Young, who has called attention to a number of references to the Servant's priestly work in this fourth Servant song (cf. 53:10–12).[54]

In conclusion, that the Servant will "sprinkle many nations" is a metonymy of cause (sprinkling) for effect (cleansing), here understood spiritually of His atoning work, which will be set forth in greater detail in chapter 53. The Servant will cleanse and purify for God's use those nations for whom His death is an expiatory satisfaction for sins.[55] Unger relates that cleansing more particularly to "millennial nations" that the Servant-Messiah will "sprinkle expiatorily and cleanse for their role (as nations) in the Davidic-Messianic earthly Kingdom (2 Sam. 7:8–15)."[56]

That "kings will shut their mouths because of him" (v. 15b) has been understood in three different senses: (1) they keep their mouths firmly closed to avoid contamination from the Servant;[57] (2) they are speechless from "their inability to say anything by

51. Young, "The Interpretation of יזה," pp. 129–31.
52. This has led some scholars to translate the verb as "spurt, scatter," so that the nations are scattered in judgment (Pieper, *Isaiah II*, pp. 432–33; Culver, *The Sufferings and the Glory*, pp. 30–31).
53. W. Kay, "Isaiah: Introduction, Commentary and Critical Notes," in C. F. Cook, ed., *The Bible Commentary* (Grand Rapids: Baker, 1981), 5:266, n. "A."
54. Young, "The Interpretation of יזה," pp. 131–132.
55. Mark A. Arrington, "The Identification of the Anonymous Servant in Isaiah 40–55" (Th.M. Thesis, Dallas Theological Seminary, 1971), p. 52.
56. Unger, *Commentary*, 2:1295.
57. North, *Second Isaiah*, p. 235; this peculiar view scarcely requires refutation.

way of self-justification";[58] and (3) they are silent in reverential awe and honor before the Servant.[59] The latter interpretation best fits the passage. The vital question, however, is whether or not those kings (and the nations they represent) are expressing trust in the Servant and His priestly purification ministry. Although Pieper claims that "there is nothing whatever in 52:15 to indicate that the gentiles come to the obedience of faith,"[60] a more positive answer is at least implied in the rest of the verse: "For what they were not told, they will see, and what they have not heard, they will understand" (v. 15c). This states the reason for Gentile astonishment. The Servant's atoning death and its significance will be comprehended by "kings" (probably synecdoche of the part for the whole, representing the nations and peoples of the earth) as the basis of their reverential awe. That comprehension and reverence includes faith in the priestly work of the Servant, as is evident in that a major point of the verse seems to be that the Servant's substitutionary death (to be described in chap. 53) is in place of Gentiles (52:15) as well as Israelites (53:1–9). Because 53:1–9 is a confession of faith on the part of a future generation of Israelites, it seems that the comprehension and awe on the part of the Gentiles in 52:15 would also include the concept of faith. The apostle Paul refers to this verse in connection with taking the gospel to those Gentiles who hear it for the first time (Rom. 15:21). But the ultimate fulfillment may relate to the Gentiles of the end time who understand and accept the message of the Servant's person and redemptive work, resulting in their salvation and entrance into the blessing of the millennial kingdom.[61]

BELIEVING ISRAELITES CONFESS THEIR PAST MISUNDERSTANDING OF THE SERVANT'S DEATH, WHICH THEY CONTRAST WITH ITS TRUE MEANING (53:1–9)

Two important issues for this passage are the identification of its speaker or speakers, and the question of its literary genre.

58. Archer, "Isaiah," p. 646.
59. Young, *Book of Isaiah*, 3:339.
60. Pieper, *Isaiah II*, p. 434.
61. Unger, *Commentary*, 2:1295.

A brief review of suggestions regarding literary genre produces a list that includes "a prophetic liturgy . . . [in] the form of a dirge" that is sung by "a chorus,"[62] "a prophetic allegory or parable of Israel's humiliation and triumph,"[63] or an individual thanksgiving (i.e., acknowledgment or declarative praise) psalm.[64] R. N. Whybray has defended the entire poem (53:1–12, but not 52:13–15) as being an individual thanksgiving psalm, not in form only but also in fact, the unusual feature in his view being that the sufferer is Deutero-Isaiah himself, who is described in the third person by a group of persons who "confess their own guilt, which was at least partly the cause for his suffering."[65] However, Westermann has more correctly recognized that the genre of the individual thanksgiving psalm "does no more than form the background" for Isaiah 53, which "contains a second strand which is closely woven into it— . . . a confession on the part of those who experienced salvation."[66]

The question of the identity of the speaker or speakers has received three general answers: (1) the Gentile kings of 52:15;[67] (2) the prophet himself as a representative either of the prophets of Israel, or of "all the heralds of the Messiah" (i.e., in both the Old and New Testaments),[68] or of the nation Israel;[69] or (3) the nation Israel (excluding the prophet)—either the exiles in Babylon,[70] or a future believing remnant of Israel.[71] In refutation of the view that the speakers are Gentiles, J. Skinner has pointed out that "the 'nations' and 'kings' [of 52:15] are surprised by the Servant's exaltation [better, atoning death] because they had not

62. Von Rad, The Message of the Prophets, pp. 222–23.
63. J. Lindblom, The Servant Songs in Deutero-Isaiah: A New Attempt to Solve an Old Problem (Lund: Lunds Universitets Arsskrift, 1951), pp. 37–51.
64. Cf. Whybray's summary of the views of J. Begrich and O. Kaiser (Thanksgiving, pp. 110–12).
65. Ibid., p. 127; cf. esp. pp. 109–39.
66. Westermann, Isaiah 40–66, p. 257.
67. Muilenburg, "Book of Isaiah," p. 614.
68. Hengstenberg, Christology of the Old Testament, abridged ed., p. 234.
69. Young, Book of Isaiah, 3:340.
70. Whybray, Isaiah 40–66, p. 171.
71. Delitzsch, Isaiah, 2:310–11; Unger, Commentary, 2:1295; Culver, The Sufferings and the Glory, p. 41; cf. Leupold, Exposition of Isaiah, 2:225; Pieper, Isaiah II, pp. 434–35 (Pieper refers only v. 1 to Isaiah speaking for the school of the prophets).

previously heard of it; whereas those who now speak (v. 1) have heard but could not believe."[72] There is substantial positive evidence for the speakers as repentant Israelites. Paul quotes Isaiah 53:1 in Romans 10:16 as a complaint against the unbelief of Israel. Also in Isaiah 53:8 it is declared that the sins for which the Servant is stricken are those of "my people," that is, Israel. Delitzsch has argued that "whenever we find a 'we' introduced abruptly in the midst of a prophecy, it is always Israel that speaks."[73] The *New International Verson* has correctly translated the verbs in 53:1-9 in the past tense, suggesting that the speakers are looking backward to the Servant's sufferings and death. H. C. Leupold paints an interesting picture: "So to speak, here we seem to hear two disciples standing on the street corner in Jerusalem reviewing the things that happened on Good Friday in the light of the better insight that came after Pentecost."[74] It should be noted with Unger, however, that the speakers "in the fullest prophetic scope [are] the remnant of Israel, who will turn in faith to the Messiah at His second advent (Zech. 12:10—13:1; Rom. 11:26)."[75]

The confessional report consists of three stanzas: (1) believing Israelites confess that their superficial estimation of the Servant led to His rejection (53:1-3); (2) they contrast their mistaken moral judgment concerning the Servant with His vicarious suffering (53:4-6); and (3) they contrast the unjust circumstances of the Servant's death with His sinless submission (53:7-9).

BELIEVING ISRAELITES CONFESS THAT THEIR SUPERFICIAL ESTIMATION OF THE SERVANT LED TO HIS REJECTION (53:1-3)

> [1]Who has believed our message
> and to whom has the arm of the LORD been revealed?

72. J. Skinner, *The Book of the Prophet Isaiah: Chapters XL-XLVI* (Cambridge: Cambridge U., 1951), p. 136.
73. Delitzsch, *Isaiah*, 2:310.
74. Leupold, *Exposition of Isaiah*, 2:225.
75. Unger, *Commentary*, 2:1295.

²He grew up before him like a tender shoot,
  and like a root out of dry ground.
 He had no beauty or majesty to attract us to him,
   nothing in his appearance that we should desire him.
³He was despised and rejected by men,
   a man of sorrows, and familiar with suffering.
 Like one from whom men hide their faces
   he was despised, and we esteemed him not.

In these verses believing Israelites confess that at first they did not properly value the Servant, that is, their superficial estimation of His humble appearance led them to reject Him. In a word, the Servant was "totally misunderstood because of His seeming insignificance."[76]

They lament that so few have experienced Yahweh's provision through the Servant (v. 1). Two rhetorical questions summarize the scarcity of true believers among Israel. The first question emphasizes that few have believed the message of salvation: "Who has believed our message?" (v. 1a). Such a question, which expects a negative answer ("few" or "none"), is used to assert that few of their nation previously responded to the message about the Servant. "Our message" can be understood as either "the message we have proclaimed,"[77] or "the message we have heard."[78] The context of rejection by the speakers (cf. v. 3, "we esteemed him not") favors the latter translation, viewing the speakers (or their ancestors) as the recipients who disbelieved the message about the true nature and purpose of the Servant's

76. Leupold, *Exposition of Isaiah*, 2:225.
77. Young thus says the message is "what we have caused to be heard" (*Book of Isaiah*, 3:341).
78. E.g., E. W. Hengstenberg, *Christology of the Old Testament and a Commentary on the Messianic Predictions* (Grand Rapids: Kregel, 1956), 2:275–76. Though incorrectly identifying the speakers as the Gentiles of 52:15, MacRae asserts that 53:1 is "not primarily a complaint by a group of prophets lamenting that their proclamation is not being generally received, but rather an exclamation by new converts who are overwhelmed by the wonder of salvation that has come to them" (*Gospel of Isaiah*, p. 134).

sufferings.[79] That the content of the message pertains to the Servant's sufferings and death at least as much as to His subsequent exaltation (including resurrection, see 53:10), rather than only to His exaltation, is seen in the parallelism with "the arm of the LORD" in verse 1b, a term speaking of Yahweh's power to save.

The second rhetorical question—"to whom has the arm of the LORD been revealed?" (v. 1b)—amplifies the first and asserts that few have experienced the power of Yahweh to save. The "arm of Yahweh" is frequently a reference to His power to save (e.g., 51:9; 52:10). Some have taken it here as a direct reference to the Servant (i.e., a messianic title or description),[80] but it is more likely either a reference to the content of "our message" (i.e., God's salvation provided through the sacrificial, substitutionary death of the Servant) or to the power of Yahweh in the Holy Spirit effecting faith in those who respond to the message (i.e., efficacious grace).[81]

The connection between 53:1 and the preceding verse (52:15) has been observed by E. W. Hengstenberg: "Those [the Gentile kings] understood what they formerly did not hear; Israel, on the contrary, does not believe what they have heard."[82]

They report that their nation was not impressed by the Servant's outward appearance (v. 2). This verse describes the humble condition of the Messiah before His sufferings as reported by the repentant Israelites of the last days. The Servant's humble surroundings held no attraction for a nation expecting a messianic King of regal splendor and military power. The Servant is first compared to a stunted plant struggling for life: "He grew up before him like a tender shoot, and like a root out of dry ground" (v. 2a). During the Servant's "hidden years" (Isa. 49:2),[83] He was known by Yahweh though unknown by the world. In fact, He was under the care and concern of Yahweh, being prepared

---

79. Westermann combines both ideas: "a thing of which they have heard . . . and, as such, tidings which they themselves have to pass on to others" (Isaiah 40–66, p. 260).
80. Kay, "Isaiah," p. 267.
81. Cf. Young, Book of Isaiah, 3:341.
82. Hengstenberg, Christology of the Old Testament, 2:276.
83. See commentary on 49:2 in chapter 3.

by Him as a Servant-Disciple (Isa. 50:4).[84] "Tender shoot" (lit. "suckling") is a horticultural term (it does not allude to a nursing child), referring to a tender twig that sprouts from the trunk or branch of a tree. It is true that the trunk from which the "tender shoot" springs is that of "the proud cedar ... of the Davidic monarchy [which] had been felled" (Ezek. 17:22),[85] though that may go beyond the purpose of the figure in this verse. "Root" is probably a synecdoche for a stem or shoot that springs from the root, and may be a messianic allusion to Isaiah 11:1. Some scholars view the "dry ground" as "the house of Jesse or of David."[86] W. Kay refers it to "the barren soil of human nature."[87] But if that part of the simile is even intended to have a specific referent, it is more likely a reference to the miserable circumstances of an enslaved nation and a corrupt age.[88]

The Servant lacked the regal splendor desirable to the nation: "He had no beauty or majesty to attract us to him, nothing in his appearance that we should desire him" (v. 2b). The Servant's lack of "beauty" (lit. "form," a term used to describe the physical attractiveness of Joseph [Gen. 39:6] and David [1 Sam. 16:18]) is neither a statement that He is naturally physically repulsive nor (in this verse) a reference to His disfigurement through His sufferings, but rather an estimation of His undesirability to the nation that misunderstood and rejected Him. "There was no kingly form, no regal majesty, no royal appearance. They wanted a king, but they got a carpenter."[89]

They report that their nation despised and devalued the Servant (v. 3). First, the servant was rejected because He was an associate

---

84. See commentary on 50:4 in chapter 4.
85. Urwick, *Servant of Jehovah*, p. 110.
86. Pieper, *Isaiah II*, p. 436.
87. Kay, "Isaiah," p. 267.
88. Delitzsch, *Isaiah*, 2:312; cf. Culver, *The Sufferings and the Glory*, p. 50.
89. Culver, *The Sufferings and the Glory*, p. 52; similarly, Pieper says, "There is nothing here of rank or position, wealth, power, or outward pomp or grandeur, nothing of what appeals to the eye of natural man as brilliant and imposing" (*Isaiah II*, p. 436); cf. Young, *Book of Isaiah*, 3:342. MacRae treats this verse in a similar fashion, indicating that "the character of Jesus was undoubtedly one of rare charm and attractiveness," but that He did not impress the speakers, whom MacRae views as the Gentile "leaders in distant nations" who would not be attracted to "a Galilean peasant" (*Gospel of Isaiah*, p. 135).

of suffering: "He was despised and rejected by men, a man of sorrows, and familiar with suffering" (v. 3a). The twofold occur-rence in this verse of the word "despised" sets the mood and expresses the theme of the verse, for the verb "despised" includes the thought of rejection (cf. Esau's birthright in Gen. 25:34). Robert D. Culver states that "despised" is "the most comprehen-sive of all the terms here, involving that complete act of the whole man when he utterly and completely refuses something."[90] The phrase "rejected by men" may mean "shunning men" (NEB has "he shrank from the sight of men"), but it is probably to be translated in a passive sense, "shunned by men."[91] It could also mean "lacking men (of rank)," that is, dignitaries avoided Him. The traditional translation, "rejected by men," probably retains the proper sense. It is highly unlikely that the Servant's descrip-tion as "a man of sorrows" and "familiar with suffering" refers to His having an illness or a disease such as leprosy.[92] Rather, it is a reference either to His association with the sick and suffering class in contrast to dignitaries, or to His sufferings on the cross.[93] The word "sorrows" can refer to "pains and sorrows of all kinds, physical and mental."[94] The phrase "familiar with suffering" is literally an "associate of grief, trouble, woe, misfortune, or evil."[95] Both "sorrows" and "suffering" are probably figurative for all kinds of pain and suffering, with particular reference to the Servant's sufferings on the cross. David F. Payne indicates that "it is difficult . . . to pinpoint any statement in the Song

90. Culver, The Sufferings and the Glory, p. 53.
91. Aston, Challenge of the Ages, p. 6.
92. Bernhard Duhm's view as summarized by North, Suffering Servant, pp. 47–48.
93. Cf. Pieper: "Before all others, the Servant was the object of suffering, sought out, so to speak, by suffering as the one object on earth to whom suffering pertained. All the suffering that pertained to this cursed world, He attracted to Himself, v. 6b. This suffering and these sorrows are not physical infirmity; they are the guilt of sin, wrath, curse, and punishment, taken from us and laid upon Him" (Isaiah II, pp. 437–38).
94. Ibid., p. 437.
95. Cf. ibid. Contrast D. Winton Thomas, who claims that the verb comes from ידע II, meaning "to be quiet, submissive," and so translates "brought low by sickness" ("A Consideration of Isaiah LIII in the Light of Recent Textual and Philological Study," Ephemerides Theologicae Lovaniensis 44 [January—March 1968]:79, 82–83).

which unequivocally refers to natural sickness" and that "there is no word in the passage which cannot be used of sufferings inflicted by human beings."[96]

Second, the Servant was despised as an object of displeasure: "Like one from whom men hide their faces he was despised, and we esteemed him not" (v. 3b). The first part of this clause is literally "as a hiding of faces from him" (or "from us"), and so has been translated "as a man who hid his face from us,"[97] or even "as one from whom God hides his face."[98] However, the context pictures the reaction of men to the Servant, so the New International Version's translation seems preferable. The word "despised" is deliberately repeated for emphasis. Culver points out the oddity that the word is used of Antiochus Epiphanes in Daniel 11:21 and so suggests that in the minds of His persecutors Jesus Christ "was in the same class with the reprobate who desecrated the holy altar with the carcass of a sow!"[99] The finality of the Servant's rejection is reflected in the words "we esteemed him not," aptly translated as "we held him of no account"[100] or "we reckoned him as nothing."[101] Thus the contemporaries of the Servant so totally despised and devalued Him that they ranked Him as "zero."

BELIEVING ISRAELITES CONTRAST THEIR MISTAKEN
MORAL JUDGMENT CONCERNING THE SERVANT
WITH HIS VICARIOUS SUFFERINGS (53:4–6)

> [4]Surely he took up our infirmities
>   and carried our sorrows,

96. Payne, "The Servant of the Lord," pp. 134–35. In possible parallel to the lament motif in both the individual lament and individual thanksgiving or declarative praise psalms, Payne notes that "the psalms of lament often present the reader with a succession of different portrayals of suffering, which make it very difficult to pin down the precise cause of the psalmist's complaint" (p. 134; cf. Westermann, Isaiah 40–66, p. 262).
97. Thomas, "Isaiah LIII," pp. 79, 83.
98. Urwick, Servant of Jehovah, pp. 115–17.
99. Culver, The Sufferings and the Glory, p. 57.
100. Thomas, "Isaiah LIII," p. 79.
101. John L. McKenzie, Second Isaiah, The Anchor Bible (Garden City, N.Y.: Doubleday, 1968), p. 129.

yet we considered him stricken by God,
  smitten by him, and afflicted.
⁵But he was pierced for our transgressions,
  he was crushed for our iniquities;
the punishment that brought us peace was upon him,
  and by his wounds we are healed.
⁶We all, like sheep, have gone astray,
  each of us has turned to his own way;
and the LORD has laid on him
  the iniquity of us all.

This strophe continues the confession of a future believing remnant of Israel that began in 53:1. In sharp contrast and strong contradiction to their pitiful misunderstanding (53:1–3), the true reason for the Servant's sufferings is now set forth. After confessing their mistaken evaluation of His sufferings (v. 4) and the substitutionary redemptive purpose of His sufferings (v. 5), believing Israelites acknowledge that the Servant bore their corporate alienation and individual guilt (v. 6).

They confess their mistaken evaluation of the Servant's sufferings (v. 4). The remnant of Israel express their realization that their previous negative estimation of the Servant is contradictory to the actual truth of His substitutionary sufferings. The word "surely," with which the verse begins, is a strong affirmation with some adversative force. It could be paraphrased, "But the truth of the matter is . . . " The verse continues, "He took up our infirmities and carried our sorrows" (v. 4a). The Hebrew word order by juxtaposition ("the sicknesses of *us he* bore") vividly contrasts the emphatic pronoun "he," which identifies the Servant, with the pronoun "our," which refers to the speakers. That contrast in pronouns characterizes the entire strophe (53:4–6) and highlights the concept of the Servant's vicarious, or substitutionary, suffering and death.

The verbs "took up" and "carried" suggest that the Servant felt the weight of the guilt and consequences of sin as a burden to be borne, a frequent concept in the Old Testament (see Gen. 4:13; Ex. 28:43; Lev. 17:16; 22:9; 24:15). The unusual feature here is that the Servant is taking on Himself the guilt and punishment of sin in a mediatorial capacity to make expiation for it. The concept of substitutionary atonement is strongly indicated in this passage,[102] though the many attempts to deny or dilute that truth are as varied as the theories of the doctrine of the atonement.[103] However, several items support the full vicarious atonement view that the Servant was not merely participating in the sufferings of others, nor simply removing their sin and sufferings, but rather that He took their sin and guilt away from them and upon Himself and bore it as a burden: (1) the significance of the verbs (in Isa. 53:4-6, 8, 11, 12); (2) their close verbal similarities to the Day of Atonement ritual (Lev. 16); [104] (3) the contrast between the pronouns "he" and "us/our" (Isa. 53:4-6; cf. vv. 8, 11-12); and (4) the specific identification of the Servant as a guilt offering (v. 10). Such an action is to be understood as a substitutionary bearing of their sin, guilt, and punishment. Thus the Servant was "suffering not His own, but an alien punishment."[105]

The terms "infirmities" and "sorrows," each of which should be identified as a metonymy of effect for cause, are used generally for all suffering that is viewed as the result of sin.[106] That does not mean that Christ became sick or infirm in a substitutionary sense or that divine healing of the body is guar-

102. Cf. Aston, *Challenge of the Ages*, p. 10.
103. Orlinsky contends that "the concept of vicarious suffering and atonement is not to be found here or anywhere else in the Bible" (H. M. Orlinsky, "The So-called 'Servant of the Lord' and 'Suffering Servant' in Second Isaiah" in *Studies on the Second Part of the Book of Isaiah*, Supplements to *Vetus Testamentum* [Leiden: E. J. Brill, 1967], p. 54). George A. F. Knight identifies the Servant's sufferings as "participative" but neither substitutionary nor penal, "endured, not *instead of* the other party, but *on his account*" (*Deutero-Isaiah: A Theological Commentary on Isaiah 40-55* [Nashville: Abingdon, 1965], p. 273). See also Whybray, *Isaiah 40-66*, p. 175. North's view suggests a "moral influence theory" of the Atonement (*Second Isaiah*, p. 238).
104. Kay lists eleven phrases that show verbal similarities to Leviticus 16 and the Day of Atonement ritual ("Isaiah," p. 266).
105. Pieper, *Isaiah II*, p. 440.
106. Young indicates that "when it is said that he bore our sicknesses, what is meant is not that he became a fellow sufferer with us, but that he bore the sin that is the cause of the evil consequences, and thus became our substitution" (*Book of Isaiah*, 3:346).

anteed through the atonement (except in the ultimate sense of a resurrection body). Matthew's citation of this verse (Matt. 8:17) in connection with Christ's miracles of healing refers to the partial removal of the effect (sickness) in view of the complete removal of the cause (sin), which would be accomplished through His death on the cross.

Having confessed their more recent realization of the true nature and cause of the Servant's sufferings, the believing remnant of Israel identifies their earlier mistaken moral judgment concerning the cause of His sufferings: "yet we considered him stricken by God, smitten by him, and afflicted" (v. 4b). Their wrong understanding was not concerning the divine agency behind the sufferings of the Servant (a fact asserted in vv. 6b, 10a) but rather in the implied reason for those sufferings—that the Servant (like Miriam or Uzziah) was suffering His own due punishment from God. Westermann points out that "this attitude was the orthodox, correct, even the devout one . . . [because] in the ancient world's way of thinking suffering as such indicated God's smiting and his wrath."[107] That is supported by the significance of the three passive participles that describe the people's estimation of the Servant's sufferings (v. 4b). The Hebrew word translated "stricken" (from נָגַע [nāga'], "to touch, smite") can mean "smite with disease," especially leprosy, often in punishment for sin (Miriam in Num. 12:9–10; Uzziah in 2 Kings 15:5). The related noun נֶגַע (nēga') is used about sixty times in Leviticus 13–14 of "leprosy" (the "stroke"). The phrase "smitten by him" (lit. "God") specifies the already implied divine source of the sufferings. The term "afflicted" may carry the meaning of inflicted or humiliated with disease (Num. 14:12; Deut. 28:22). All three expressions—"stricken by God, smitten by him, and afflicted"—are used figuratively of the Servant to depict the severity of the consequences of His bearing the sin of others in a substitutionary capacity.

Thus, believing Israelites now recognize that the Servant bore the consequences of their sin, whereas they once thought that He deserved the sufferings He received.

107. Westermann, Isaiah 40–66, pp. 262–63.

They recognize the substitutionary redemptive purpose of the Servant's sufferings (v. 5). The vicarious purpose of the sufferings of the Servant, recognized in v. 4, is amplified in this verse. The Servant's sufferings were the penalty for their sins: "But he was pierced for our transgressions, he was crushed for our iniquities" (v. 5a). The opening conjunction may be taken in either an adversative sense ("but")[108] or an adverbial sense ("while").[109] In either case, the clause draws a contrast between the real design of the Servant's sufferings and the apparent cause of His sufferings as it had been perceived by the speakers (v. 4b). The verb "pierced" is one of the strongest words in the Hebrew language to describe a violent and painful death.[110] "Pierced" conveys the idea of "pierced through," or "wounded to death" (cf. Deut. 21:1; Isa. 51:9; see also Ps. 22:16; Zech. 12:10; John 19:34). The related adjective (חָלָל [ḥālāl]) usually means "slain" (Isa. 22:2; 34:3; 66:16). "Crushed" (דָּכָא [dākā']) literally means "broken to pieces, shattered." However, the verb consistently is used (except in Deut. 23:1) in a metaphorical sense, such as a "crushed spirit" (Isa. 57:15) or a "crushed heart" (Ps. 51:17). Even David's petition "Let the bones you have crushed rejoice" (Ps. 51:8) is clearly a figurative reference to emotional rather than physical crushing.[111] Isaiah here uses the verb "crushed" in a parallel construction to "pierced" (which refers to the Servant's physical death). Although it is possible that "crushed" also refers to His physical death (though not to literal "crushing" as with stones), it is more likely (to be consistent with Old Testament usage) that it refers to His emotional destruction in bearing sin as a substitute for guilty sinners. Thus it is related to His death but describing the emotional rather than physical aspects of His

108. Urwick, *Servant of Jehovah*, p. 122.
109. Dewbury, "Exegetical Study," p. 37. If taken adverbially, the circumstantial clause portrays vividly the greatness of their misunderstanding— that they were thinking wrongly at the same time the Servant was suffering vicariously.
110. So Urwick, *Servant of Jehovah*, p. 123; contrast the view of Driver, "Isaiah 52:13—53:12," p. 94.
111. G. Johannes Botterweck and Helmer Ringgren, eds., *Theological Dictionary of the Old Testament* (Grand Rapids: Eerdmans, 1974), 3:195-208.

death sufferings. The burden of sin, guilt, and punishment that He bore is described in terms of "our transgressions" (i.e., "rebellions"; cf. 1 Kings 12:19; Isa. 1:2; 43:27) and "our iniquities" (including guilt).

Turning from the bearing of sin, the speakers affirm that the Servant's sufferings were the means of their spiritual restoration: "the punishment that brought us peace was upon him, and by his wounds we are healed" (v. 5b). The *New International Version* translation "punishment" is preferred over the King James Version's "chastisement," which is too weak a term because it here procures "peace," indicating that the justice of God is involved.[112] "Peace" refers not to cessation of war but to the removal of the barrier of sin, which caused enmity with God (cf. Rom. 5:1; Eph. 2:14-18; Col. 1:20). The punishment was "upon him," again indicating His substitutionary bearing of sin and guilt. The term "wounds" is a collective noun referring to His suffering in a general way. As the "peace" is spiritual rather than physical, so also is the "healing" that results from "his wounds." "As the punishment of sin and suffering are often represented under the image of a disease, so is deliverance from them under that of healing."[113]

This verse contributes significantly to the language of substitutionary atonement found in Isaiah 53. "Nothing can be stronger than the antithesis running through this verse, both between the pronouns *he, him, his,* on the one hand, and *our, our, our, us,* on the other; and that between the wounding, bruising, chastisement, stripes on the one hand, and the *peace* and *healing* on the other."[114]

They acknowledge that the Servant bore their corporate alienation and individual guilt (v. 6). Before affirming what Yahweh has done with their guilt, the believing remnant of Israel compare their corporate alienation and individual guilt to the waywardness of sheep: "We all, like sheep, have gone astray, each of us has

112. Delitzsch, *Isaiah,* 2:318-19.
113. Hengstenberg, *Christology of the Old Testament,* abridged ed., p. 236.
114. Urwick, *Servant of Jehovah,* p. 125; on the nature of vicarious substitution in this passage, see Young, *Book of Isaiah,* 3:347-48.

turned to his own way" (v. 6a). This verse clearly corrects any misconception about why the Servant suffered. The *New International Version* very accurately retains the Hebrew word order regarding the inclusion formed by the emphatic "all" (כֻּלָּנוּ [*kullānû*], "all of us") at the beginning and ending of the verse. That emphasizes the fact that those whose iniquity was borne by the Servant are identical to those who have corporately and individually wandered away like sheep. That fact was true of all Israel ("all" went astray), not just the elect. Thus, at least with respect to Israel, the verse teaches an unlimited atonement. Because the context of the entire Servant song indicates that the Servant's priestly ministry is also in behalf of Gentiles (52:15), a doctrine of unlimited atonement is supported by this passage.[115] Such a provision, of course, does not mean that all will be saved (universalism).

"Gone astray" refers not to the Exile in Babylon but to wandering in the wilderness of sin (cf. Ps. 119:176). The verb is used elsewhere of Israel's spiritual aberration (Ps. 95:10; 2 Chron. 33:9; Ezek. 44:10) and occurs frequently in Isaiah (3:12; 9:16; 19:13; 47:15; 63:17). The simile "like sheep" pictures Israel as having no shepherd (cf. Num. 27:17) and includes the ideas of unawareness and helplessness. What Israel confesses concerning herself particularly surely arises from the human condition of universal sinfulness and so applies to all mankind generally.[116] In the phrase "each of us" the confession turns from the flock to the individual sheep, for although the alienation from God is universal, its manifestation is as varied as the individual number of sinners. That each individual "turned to his own way" means they were all in opposition to God's ways (cf. Isa. 40:3; 55:7-9), and thus this is very nearly a description of the essence of sin.

The believing remnant next affirm that Yahweh cast their guilt on the Servant: "and the LORD has laid on him the iniquity

---

115. This is disputed by Young, who states that "it is not warranted to draw from these words a doctrine of universal atonement" (*Book of Isaiah*, 3:350).

116. Knight agrees that "this verse surely describes the manner in which humanity as such behaves" (*Deutero Isaiah*, p. 235).

of us all" (v. 6b). All the sin and guilt (with the punishment due on it because of Israel's corporate and individual wandering in sin) was "laid on" the Servant. The verb usually denotes a violent hostile action (but contrast Isa. 64:5, "Come to the help of"; 59:16, "one to intercede"), in the sense of either "to fall or strike upon," so as to slay (2 Sam. 1:15; 1 Kings 2:25, 34, 46; but contrast Isa. 64:5; 59:16) or "to cause to converge upon." It more likely means the former, picturing human sin and guilt as coming on the Servant like a destroying foe and overwhelming Him with its wrath. However, if it means the latter, it pictures the fiery rays of judgment that should have fallen on sinners individually but were deflected and converged on Him. T. R. Birks portrays the scene as "many shafts aimed at one common target" so that "each sin of every sinner would be like a separate wound in the heart of the Man of sorrows."[117]

The astounding assertion in this verse is that believing Israel recognizes the divine agency behind the Servant's bearing of sin. Men could crucify Him, but only Yahweh could cause iniquity to strike down on Him so that He bears it in a mediatorial capacity.

BELIEVING ISRAELITES CONTRAST THE UNJUST CIRCUMSTANCES
OF THE SERVANT'S DEATH WITH HIS SINLESS SUBMISSION (53:7-9)

> [7]He was oppressed and afflicted,
>   yet he did not open his mouth;
> he was led like a lamb to the slaughter,
>   and as a sheep before her shearers is silent,
>   so he did not open his mouth.
> [8]By oppression and judgment, he was taken away.
>   And who can speak of his descendants?
> For he was cut off from the land of the living;
>   for the transgression of my people he was stricken.
> [9]He was assigned a grave with the wicked,
>   and with the rich in his death,

117. T. R. Birks, *Commentary on the Book of Isaiah* (London: Rivingtons, 1871), p. 270.

> though he had done no violence,
> nor was any deceit in his mouth.

These verses continue the Israelite remnant's report regarding the sufferings and death of Yahweh's Servant. An alternate view that the prophet Isaiah becomes the speaker in this strophe (in part or in total)[118] does not affect the content or significance of the description, namely, that the mistreated Servant silently submitted Himself to death (v. 7), a death that His contemporaries did not understand (v. 8) and that was followed by an honorable burial despite the intention of His enemies (v. 9).

The mistreated Servant silently submitted Himself to death (v. 7). The remnant of believing Israelites report that the Servant patiently endured mistreatment: "He was oppressed and afflicted, yet he did not open his mouth" (v. 7a). This verse highlights the patient submissiveness of Yahweh's innocent Servant in the face of mistreatment. Of the various meanings of the Hebrew נָגַשׂ (*nāgaś*, "press, drive, oppress, exact"[119]), it probably does not mean "exact" (which would make the maltreatment of the Servant like that of "an unrelenting creditor"; cf. Deut. 15:2–3)[120] but rather "oppressed" in the sense of mistreatment in general. The clause וְהוּא נַעֲנֶה (*wᵉhû' na'ᵃneh*) appears to be a circumstantial clause ("while he was afflicted" or "while he afflicted himself" [if the Niphal has a reflexive force]),[121] although some scholars see only an emphatic force in וְהוּא (*wᵉhû'*, "and he"). The Servant's voluntary submission to suffering is further stressed in that in spite of His maltreatment "he did not open his mouth" (cf. Matt. 26:63; 27:12–14; Mark 15:5; Luke 23:9; John 19:9). He did not confess any sin nor did He protest His innocence. He simply suffered silently, in submission to the will of Yahweh. That silence of submission pertains to the legal accusations against Him and is not inconsistent with "the Lord's re-

---

118. See the discussion on "my people" in verse 8.
119. Francis Brown, Samuel R. Driver, and Charles A. Briggs, *A Hebrew and English Lexicon of the Old Testament* (Oxford: Clarendon, 1955), p. 620.
120. Kay, *Isaiah*, p. 269.
121. North, *Second Isaiah*, p. 240.

sponses to the high priest or to the secular court, or to what He said to Judas or to the soldiers in the garden."[122]

In contrast to the wandering sheep of Isaiah 53:6, the Servant "was led like a lamb to the slaughter, and as a sheep before her shearers is silent, so he did not open his mouth" (v. 7b). The entire simile ("like a lamb to the slaughter") probably refers both to the lamb and to the Servant.[123] Although the parallel clause "as a sheep before her shearers" could suggest that the slaughter is commercial in nature, yet the sacrificial scope of the context indicates that the "slaughter" is sacrificial in nature. Thus the thought is that the Servant voluntarily submitted to sacrificial death, a meaning supported by the context (cf. 1 Pet. 1:18–19).

The Servant's contemporaries did not understand the meaning of His death (v. 8). The unjust condemnation of the Servant is expressed in the words "By oppression and judgment, he was taken away" (v. 8a). "By oppression and judgment" may be translated and interpreted several ways. Most of the possibilities suggest violent action against the Servant within a legal context.[124] Driver has translated the phrase, "Without protection (of kin) and without due legal procedure;"[125] the idea is that no attempt was made to secure a fair trial for the Servant. Some scholars regard the nouns as a hendiadys, meaning "by reason of an oppressive sentence," or "a perverted judgment," or alternately "judicial violence."[126] However, Payne is probably correct that there is "some fixed legal idiom here, either 'after arrest and sentence' or 'from prison and lawcourt.'"[127] Calvin understood the next phrase ("he was taken away") to refer to rescue by resurrection (i.e., taken away into glory).[128] However, the general sense must be "dragged to punishment,"[129] but not merely to

---

122. Pieper, *Isaiah II*, p. 444.
123. Payne, "The Servant of the Lord," pp. 134–35.
124. Westermann, *Isaiah 40–66*, p. 265.
125. Driver, "Isaiah 52:13—53:12," p. 94.
126. North, *Second Isaiah*, p. 241; McKenzie, *Second Isaiah*, p. 130; Pieper, *Isaiah II*, p. 446.
127. Payne, "The Servant of the Lord," p. 139.
128. John Calvin, *Isaiah*, vol. 3 of *Calvin's Commentaries* (reprint, Grand Rapids: Associated Publishers and Authors, n.d.), p. 728.
129. Hengstenberg, *Christology of the Old Testament*, abridged ed., p. 238.

"take away to prison," like the Israelites to exile (52:5).[130] In the light of the context, it is a reference to the Servant's being "hurried away to death."[131] Culver understands it as a reference to "hurried, forcible, violent treatment, resulting in death."[132] In summary, the Servant "was the victim of a judicial murder."[133]

The translation of the next colon is debatable, hinging in part on the meaning of the Hebrew word דּוֹר (dôr). Some scholars have taken this word (usually by emending the text) in the sense of "fate," "plight," or "what befell him."[134] John L. McKenzie emends the noun to דָּבָר (dābār) and translates it as "case," to fit in with the judicial context in the preceding colon.[135] Scholars who accept the reading of the Masoretic text choose between the translations "descendants"[136] (NIV text) and "generation"[137] (NIV margin), that is, "contemporaries." The translation of the remainder of the verse given in the *New Internatinal Version* margin is to be preferred: "Yet who of his generation considered that he was cut off from the land of the living for the transgression of my people, to whom the blow was due?"[138] Thus the meaning of the verse is this: although the Servant was unjustly condemned, the Servant's contemporaries did not understand the meaning of His death. The meaning of "cut off" suggests a violent, premature, and unnatural death,[139] though the term does

130. Whybray, *Isaiah 40–66*, p. 177.
131. Urwick, *Servant of Jehovah*, p. 137; Young, *Book of Isaiah*, 3:351.
132. Culver, *The Sufferings and the Glory*, p. 92.
133. MacRae, *Gospel of Isaiah*, p. 140.
134. Thomas, "Isaiah LIII," p. 84; North, *Second Isaiah*, p. 230; Driver, "Isaiah 52:13—53:12," p. 95; Leupold, *Exposition of Isaiah*, 2:230.
135. McKenzie, *Second Isaiah*, p. 130.
136. If the reference is to physical descendants, the idea is that He was cut off prematurely, before the normal cycle of producing progeny. However, some scholars take the reference to spiritual progeny, the rhetorical question affirming their innumerable quantity.
137. Urwick refers "generation" to the Servant's own "generation," that is, origin: "none fully *estimated* the Redeemer's generation, in its widest sense . . . as to its origin . . . as to His earthly life, as to His character, perfect in holiness, and . . . as to His everlasting reign" (*Servant of Jehovah*, p. 139).
138. For a defense of this general line of translation, see Pieper, *Isaiah II*, p. 446.
139. Compare Hengstenberg, *Christology of the Old Testament*, abridged ed., p. 239.

not indicate the exact cause of death. The violence indicated by the word is suggested through a translation such as "forcibly removed" or "wrenched."[140] The addition of "from the land of the living" eliminates any doubt as to the fact of the Servant's death (cf. Isa. 38:11; Ezek. 32:22–32). Whybray's attempt to regard the phrase as metaphorical of Deutero-Isaiah's suffering[141] (a literary device found in the lament and thanksgiving psalms) is out of harmony with the clear thrust of the passage.

The term "my people" clearly distinguishes the Servant from Israel, but to whom does the pronoun "my" refer? The singular pronoun "my" seems to interrupt the preceding report by a group of speakers who identify themselves by plural pronouns. That has led scholars to adopt various devices to explain the change. Apart from various emendations of the text,[142] several approaches have been suggested. Joseph A. Alexander regards the singular pronoun as conveying a plural meaning (cf. 1 Sam. 5:10, "to kill us and our people" [Heb., "to kill me and my people"]), so that the speakers really mean "our people."[143] Some scholars refer the pronoun directly to God.[144] The pronoun is referred to the prophet Isaiah by others, such as Leupold, who states: "A momentary personal note enters the picture when the prophet observes the fact that it was his own people ('my people') that were the beneficiaries of this strange transaction."[145] Because the term "people" refers unambiguously to Israel, the identity of the pronominal reference affects only the form or structure of the verse, not its significance, which supports the Servant's substitutionary death for the nation. That the "blow was due" (NIV margin) Israel but fell on the Servant (cf. vv. 4–7) reaffirms one more time the substitutionary nature of the

---

140. North, *Second Isaiah*, p. 241; Knight, *Deutero-Isaiah*, p. 236.
141. Whybray, *Isaiah 40–66*, p. 177; cf. Westermann, *Isaiah 40–66*, p. 265.
142. Several emendations are noted in Muilenberg, "Book of Isaiah," 5:626; the Dead Sea Scroll 1QIsᵃ reads עַמּוֹ (*'ammô*, "his people"), but this lacks other textual support.
143. Alexander, *Commentary*, 2:300.
144. Kay, "Isaiah," p. 268; Young, *Book of Isaiah*, 3:352.
145. Leupold, *Exposition of Isaiah*, 2:230.

Servant's death, which was not comprehended by most of His contemporaries.

The innocent Servant received an honorable burial despite the intent of His enemies (v. 9). The description of the Servant's sufferings and death moves on to the facts of His burial. The intention of the Servant's enemies went unfulfilled in view of His honorable burial: "He was assigned a grave with the wicked, and [or, 'but he was'] with the rich in his death" (v. 9a). Because they were crucifying the Servant with wicked men, it would be expected that He would be buried with them. Christopher R. North points out:

> It was usual for a man to be buried "with his fathers," and to be denied such a burial was a calamity (1 Kings xiii. 22). For those who had no family grave there was the common burial place (2 Kings xxiii. 6; Jer. xxvi. 23; cf. Matt. xxvii. 7). Whether some part of this was reserved for criminals we do not know, unless it may be inferred from this passage.[146]

Several problems arise in the next colon. Is *waw* a conjunctive ("and") or an adversative ("but")? That is, is the second colon synonymous or antithetical to the first colon? Many scholars regard the parallelism as synonymous, viewing "wicked" and "rich" as synonymous terms.[147] However, Urwick points out that there is "no intimation of character" in the word "rich."[148] The phrase "in his death" obviously refers to after dying (cf. Lev. 11:31; 1 Kings 13:31), that is, "in his burial," but there is no need to revocalize the text with McKenzie and others to get "his tomb."[149] It is preferable to understand the parallelism as antithetical: they appointed His grave with wicked men, but He was actually buried in a rich man's tomb (cf. Matt. 27:57–60).[150] The

146. North, *Second Isaiah*, p. 241.
147. P. A. H. De Boer states, "The expression 'a rich man,' probably meant collectively, is a synonym of the wicked; compare the Book of Psalms wherein the wicked, the rich men are the enemies of the pious people" (*Second-Isaiah's Message* [Leiden: E. J. Brill, 1956], p. 114).
148. Urwick, *Servant of Jehovah*, p. 145.
149. McKenzie, *Second Isaiah*, p. 131.
150. See Young, *Book of Isaiah*, 3:353, n. 34.

implication of the passage is that Yahweh overrules the intentions of men and ordains that His Servant will have a splendid tomb.[151] "The reason for His honorable sepulture [i.e., burial], so different from what His foes had planned, was that after His redemptive work had been accomplished, the Lord allowed no more indignities to be perpetrated upon Him."[152]

The *New International Version* translates the next line concessively, affirming that men rejected Him, "although he had done no violence, nor was any deceit in his mouth" (v. 9*b*).[153] It is more probably causal, indicating the cause of Yahweh's providential overturning of men's purposes: "because he had done no violence."[154] On no "deceit" being in his mouth, see 1 Peter 2:22.

This strophe, in which the unjust circumstances of the Servant's death are contrasted with His sinless submission, concludes the confessional report of believing Israelites, a report anticipating the repentance of Israel at the second advent of Christ (cf. Zech. 12:10—13:1).

Yahweh Promises to Exalt His Servant Because He Did His Will in Dying as a Guilt Offering (53:10–12)

[10]Yet it was the LORD'S will to crush him and cause him to suffer,
    and though the LORD makes his life a guilt offering,
he will see his offspring and prolong his days,
    and the will of the LORD will prosper in his hand.
[11]After the suffering of his soul,
    he will see the light of life and be satisfied;
by his knowledge my righteous servant will justify many,
    and he will bear their iniquities.
[12]Therefore I will give him a portion among the great,
    and he will divide the spoils with the strong,
because he poured out his life unto death,
    and was numbered with the transgressors.

151. Pieper, *Isaiah II*, p. 448; but cf. Urwick, *Servant of Jehovah*, p. 147.
152. Unger, *Commentary*, 2:1299.
153. See Urwick, *Servant of Jehovah*, p. 147.
154. Delitzsch, *Isaiah*, 2:326, 329; Young, *Book of Isaiah*, 3:353.

For he bore the sin of many,
   and made intercession for the transgressors.

As the fourth Servant song begins with a divine oracle in which Yahweh announces the exaltation of His Servant (52:13–15), so it climaxes with a divine oracle in which Yahweh again promises the Servant's exaltation (53:10–12). "The revolutionary truth announced in these verses is that the servant's vindication comes after his death. A great miracle takes place, therefore, for after his death and burial he is enabled to see his offspring, to prolong his days, and to witness the successful completion of his mission."[155]

The promise of Yahweh is introduced by a declaration in which Isaiah reveals that the will of Yahweh is accomplished through the sacrificial death and subsequent exaltation of the Servant (53:10). In the oracle proper Yahweh promises first that His Servant will justify many as a result of His knowledge and suffering (53:11) and second that His Servant will have victorious dominion because He died bearing the sins of many (53:12).

ISAIAH REVEALS THAT THE WILL OF YAHWEH
IS ACCOMPLISHED IN THE SACRIFICIAL DEATH AND
SUBSEQUENT EXALTATION OF THE SERVANT (53:10)

The Servant suffers and dies as a guilt offering according to the will of Yahweh (v. 10a). Isaiah indicates that the Servant's suffering and sacrificial death are within the will of Yahweh: "it was the LORD's will to crush him and cause him to suffer, and . . . the LORD makes his life a guilt offering." Men could inflict suffering and death on the Servant, but only Yahweh could make His life a guilt offering, thus making the wrath of men serve His merciful purpose (cf. 1 Pet. 1:20; Acts 2:23).[156] Culver correctly observes that "the divine plan and purpose are in view rather than divine

155. Kelley, "Isaiah," p. 344.
156. Urwick, Servant of Jehovah, p. 148; Pieper, Isaiah II, p. 449. Young points out that "this does not absolve from responsibility those who put him to death, but they were not in control of the situation" (Book of Isaiah, 3:354).

enjoyment."[157] The two verbs may be a hendiadys meaning "to bruise him painfully."[158] The reference is directly to the dying sufferings of the Servant (cf. the treatment of "crushed" in v. 5).

Controversy arises as to the subject of the verb תָּשִׂים (tāśîm), which could be second person singular ("you make," NIV margin) or third feminine singular (agreeing in gender with the noun נַפְשׁוֹ (napshô, "his life" or "soul"). If the verb is second person ("you make"), the undesignated antecedent of the pronoun must be Yahweh (so the NIV translates "the LORD makes"). Although Yahweh has just been referred to in the third person, so that this change to the second person is abrupt, it is not unparalleled in prophetic literature.[159] In fact, this sudden address to Yahweh can be compared to the previous use of apostrophe in 52:14, where Yahweh abruptly addresses the Servant—the two cases of apostrophe in the epilogue and prologue forming a kind of literary inclusio.[160] Therefore the *New International Version* margin gives the most accurate translation: "You [Yahweh] make his life [i.e., the Servant] a guilt offering."[161]

Offered as such by the Servant and accepted as such by Yahweh, the Servant poured out His life in death as "a guilt offering." The guilt offering was one of the basic Levitical sacrifices (cf. Lev. 5:14—6:7; 7:1-6). It was required when one deprived another (whether God or man) of his rightful due. It normally occasioned a restitution payment and fine to the party wronged. The ram of the guilt offering was not part of the restitution but was an expiation for the sin before God (Lev. 5:15, 18; 6:6; 19:20). The results of the guilt offering included atonement and forgiveness (Lev. 5:16). Although some scholars

---

157. Culver, *The Sufferings and the Glory*, p. 107.
158. Young, *Book of Isaiah*, 3:354, n. 37.
159. Kelley's view that the "you" is "the worshiper who must appropriate the servant's sacrifice and make it the means of his approach to God" is even more abrupt and lacks contextual confirmation ("Isaiah," 5:344).
160. Kenneth L. Barker, personal correspondence, June 7, 1982.
161. On the other hand, Urwick says, "His soul" is "not simply for the pronoun, but with special reference to the nature of the 'āshām, which was the guilt offering in the case of individual sin" (*Servant of Jehovah*, pp. 151-52); Thomas repoints the verb as a passive and translates, "Though his own life be made an offering for sin" ("Isaiah LIII," p. 85).

view the reference to the guilt offering in Isaiah 53:10 as merely a generic reference to the sacrificial system,[162] the term probably emphasizes Christ's expiatory death as an atonement for the damage or injury done by sin. In either case, the passage clearly points to the sacrificial character of the Servant's death as a satisfaction of divine justice and a foundation for forgiveness.

The Servant triumphs after death to advance the will of Yahweh (v. 10b). After declaring that the Servant accomplished the will of Yahweh by offering Himself as a guilt offering, Isaiah discloses that the Servant will triumph after death: "he will see his offspring and prolong his days, and the will of the LORD will prosper in his hand." Payne is correct in saying that "Isaiah 53 contains no plain statement of resurrection, and one does not know by what process the prophet envisaged death as giving place to life."[163] However, there is a strong implication of resurrection not only because the Servant "will see his offspring" after He has died, but also because He will "prolong his days," that is, enjoy long life in spite of having given his life as a guilt offering. Although it is correct that "long life and numerous descendants are regarded by the Hebrews as the highest prosperity, as a theocratic blessing and a reward of piety,"[164] the passage does not explicitly state that the life and offspring are given to the Servant as a reward (but cf. v. 12).[165]

The verse concludes as it began—with an affirmation concerning the efficient accomplishment of the purpose of Yahweh through His Servant, that "by His mediation, God's purpose is

162. MacRae states, "The suggestion has been made that various other sacrifices prescribed in the book of Leviticus might seem better to fit the meaning of the atonement than this particular one (called a sin offering in the KJV). The answer may well be that this offering stands here as representing the entire sacrificial system, which finds its fulfillment in the voluntary death of the Servant of the LORD" (*Gospel of Isaiah,* pp. 144–45); Young says that "the word stands generally for expiatory sacrifice" (*Book of Isaiah,* 3:354).

163. Payne, "The Servant of the Lord," p. 139.

164. Hengstenberg, *Christology of the Old Testament,* abridged ed., p. 240.

165. Pieper is representative of those scholars who stress that because the Servant brings the guilt offering, eternal life and His spiritual seed accrue to Him as a reward (*Isaiah II,* pp. 450–51).

completely accomplished."[166] As He did with Joseph in Egypt (Gen. 39:3-4), so Yahweh will cause the Servant to be successful in all His undertakings.

YAHWEH PROMISES THAT HIS SERVANT WILL JUSTIFY MANY AS A RESULT OF HIS KNOWLEDGE AND SUFFERING (53:11)

Yahweh now affirms that the Servant will have satisfaction after suffering (v. 11a) and that the Servant will justify many (v. 11b).

The Servant will have satisfaction after suffering (v. 11a). Pieper views verses 11-12 as an amplification of the clause "he will see his offspring" (v. 10).[167] The validity of that view depends on the interpretation of "he will see" in verse 11 and "a portion" in verse 12. In any case the Servant's postmortem satisfaction includes more than seeing His spiritual offspring. Death does not spell defeat for the Servant, for "after the suffering of his soul, he will see the light of life and be satisfied." Although the *New International Version* translates the preposition in a temporal sense ("after"),[168] it seems also to include an element of causality ("because of").[169] However, the temporal element must not be minimized, for the "seeing" is subsequent to the "suffering," that is, it is after the Servant's death. Urwick's suggestion that the cross is "the point from which he looks and is satisfied"[170] misses the point of the sequence.

But what is the object of the verb "he will see"? The Hebrew Masoretic text lacks the phrase translated "the light of life." That translation is supported in part ("light") by the Dead Sea Scrolls and the LXX. The *New International Version* margin translates the Masoretic text as follows: "he will see the result of the suffering of his soul and be satisfied." Hengstenberg identifies the implied object as "the fruits and rewards of his sufferings."[171]

166. Unger, *Commentary*, 2:1300.
167. Pieper, *Isaiah II*, p. 452.
168. See Urwick, *Servant of Jehovah*, p. 154 ("after the suffering, glory").
169. Young, *Book of Isaiah*, 3:356; Pieper, *Isaiah II*, p. 452.
170. Urwick, *Servant of Jehovah*, p. 154.
171. Hengstenberg, *Christology of the Old Testament*, abridged ed., p. 241.

More properly it looks back to "his offspring" (v. 10) as well as forward to the "many" who are justified (v. 11b).[172] Young views the verbs "see" and "be satisfied" as a hendiadys meaning "he shall see with abundant satisfaction," but Hengstenberg more correctly separates them as forming a climax.[173] High spiritual satisfaction follows the most profound depths of the Servant's suffering.

The Servant will justify many (v. 11b). Yahweh's promise, "By his knowledge my righteous servant will justify many," has been the subject of much debate, with attention focused especially on the means of this justification stated in the phrase "by his knowledge." The question has been precisely stated by John Murray: "Is the knowledge subjective or objective in respect [to] the person in view? Is it the knowledge the Servant possesses, his own knowledge (subjective) or is it the knowledge others possess of him, knowledge of him (objective)?"[174] Hengstenberg, with many scholars, views the knowledge as objective, claiming that the topic is "not the procuring of righteousness but only the conferring of it."[175] Likewise Young maintains, "Not by his knowledge does he justify men, but by bearing their iniquities."[176] Alexander similarly states: "The only satisfactory construction . . . makes the phrase mean, *by knowledge of him* upon the part of others; and this is determined by the whole connection to mean practical experimental knowledge, involving faith and a self-appropriation of the Messiah's righteousness."[177]

On the alternate side, Delitzsch has argued for the subjective sense of the Servant's own knowledge, comparing it to the

172. Urwick regards "his seed" (v. 10, "offspring," NIV) as the implied object of the verb "see" (*Servant of Jehovah*, p. 154). Barker views the object as both the "offspring" (v. 10) and the "many" (v. 11) (personal correspondence, June 7, 1982).

173. Young, *Book of Isaiah*, 3:356; Hengstenberg, *Christology of the Old Testament*, abridged ed., p. 241.

174. John Murray, *The Epistle to the Romans: The English Text with Introduction, Exposition and Notes*, 2 vols. (Grand Rapids: Eerdmans, 1959, 1965), 1:375. Murray's "Appendix C—Isaiah 53:11" (1:375–83) is a very helpful treatment of this problem.

175. Hengstenberg, *Christology of the Old Testament*, abridged ed., p. 241.

176. Young, *Book of Isaiah*, 3:357.

177. Alexander, *Commentary*, 2:305; see also Unger, *Commentary*, 2:1300.

priestly knowledge referred to in Malachi 2:7.[178] The most adequate statement of the subjective view of this phrase has been given by Murray:

> There are numerous respects in which knowledge may be viewed an essential part of the equipment of the righteous Servant in the expiatory acomplishment which is the burden of the passage. . . . From whatever angle the task assigned to him and perfected by him as the Servant of the Lord may be viewed, knowledge is an indispensable ingredient of the obedience which his servanthood entailed. . . . His own knowledge can therefore be conceived of as not only relevant to the Servant's justifying action but also as indispensable to its discharge, whether the action is that of his once-for-all expiatory accomplishment or that of his continual work [in actual justification] as the exalted Lord.

Thus Murray concludes that Isaiah is speaking of "the Servant's own knowledge in all the reaches of its reference as it applies to the work of the Servant as the sin-bearer, as the trespass [guilt] offering, and as the high priest offering himself."[179]

It is difficult to determine how Isaiah understood "his knowledge." As a whole the passage is speaking of the Servant's work of substitutionary atonement. Apart from the implied faith on the part of the speakers of 53:1-9, there is no direct reference to the appropriation of the Servant's expiation. Yet it is questionable if one should go all the way with Murray and regard justification here as "the virtual synonym of expiation," with no reference at all to, as Murray calls it, "actual [subjective] justification."[180] Rather, the word play in the Hebrew (צַדִּיק צַדִּיק [yaṣdîq ṣādîq]) supports the identification of this justification as forensic and actual: "My *righteous* Servant will declare many *righteous*."[181]

---

178. Delitzsch, *Isaiah*, 2:337; cf. Arrington, "Identification of the Anonymous Servant," pp. 52-53. Barker suggests that such a priestly knowledge may be referred to in 52:13a and may be actually exercised in 52:15a (personal correspondence, June 7, 1982).
179. Murray, *Romans*, 1:379-80.
180. Ibid., p. 381.
181. Barker, personal correspondence, June 7, 1982.

The verse concludes with another reference to the Servant's substitutionary work for Israel and the nations: "he will bear their iniquities" (v. 11c). It is the Servant's action toward the "all" as previously described in verses 4–6 that is the foundation for the justification of "many." The "all" whose iniquities are borne by the Servant (vv. 4–6) include the "many" who are actually justified (v. 11).

YAHWEH PROMISES THAT HIS SERVANT WILL HAVE VICTORIOUS DOMINION BECAUSE HE DIED BEARING THE SINS OF MANY (53:12)

The Servant will receive the reward of the Victor (v. 12a). The promise of Yahweh to exalt His Servant supremely is cast into a description drawn from the reward given to a victorious warrior following military conquest: "Therefore I will give him a portion among the great, and he will divide the spoils with the strong." "The military idea of dividing spoil may be taken either in a literal fashion, with the Servant seen as participating in world government, or in a metaphorical sense, describing the Servant's spiritual conquests."[182] The term "portion" designates not "a part" but "the appointed portion, the lot, the inheritance."[183] The picture is that of the triumphant Servant-Messiah, surrounded by the righteous ones who share His triumph, particularly the "kings"/"nations" of 52:15 and the "offspring" of 53:10. However, some view the Servant as dividing the spoils with His enemies rather than with His followers: "As a result of Christ's atonement, He will rescue many from the control of Satan and his strong and powerful forces."[184] But that does not seem to fit the sense of the metaphors used here.

The Servant gave His life for sinners (v. 12b,c). The basis of the Servant's inheritance or reward is identified by Yahweh: "because he poured out his life unto death, and was numbered with the transgressors [cf. Matt. 27:38; Luke 22:37]. For he bore the sin of many [cf. Mark 10:45], and made intercession for the transgressors." This passage draws the strophe to a conclusion in

182. Dewbury, "Exegetical Study," p. 53.
183. Pieper, *Isaiah II*, p. 455.
184. MacRae, *Gospel of Isaiah*, p. 147.

ideas similar to those expressed throughout the fourth Servant song, thus emphasizing His satisfactory substitutionary sacrifice for sinners. The one statement requiring further comment is the final clause, "made intercession for the transgressors." Although Christ made intercession for transgressors while He was dying on the cross ("Father, forgive them . . . " [Luke 23:34]), the term here may refer to His continual high priestly intercession for His own (John 17; Heb. 7:25; cf. Isa. 62:1, 6–7). Yet in view of the emphasis in the context on His expiatory death, it is possible that the intercession described is more than verbal and so refers to the fact that He intervened by His death for transgressors. North says that "the figure is of the Servant placing himself between the transgressors and the punishment they deserved."[185]

CONCLUSION

Isaiah 52:13–53:12 presents the details and purpose of the Servant's sufferings and death, particularly as they relate to His exaltation and the ultimate success of His mission. The message of the song is clear: Yahweh announces the exaltation of His Servant because of His satisfactory substitutionary sacrificial death for the sins of both His guilty people and the Gentiles. The passage consists of five strophes, the central three of which compose the body of the report. Thus the song consists of three basic units: (1) an introductory appraisal in which Yahweh promises to supremely exalt His Servant, who though deeply degraded will both purify and receive the worship of nations (52:13–15); (2) a confessional report in which believing Israelites contrast their past rejection of the Servant with the true meaning of His death (53:1–9); and (3) a concluding epilogue in which Yahweh promises to exalt His Servant because He did His will in dying as a guilt offering (53:10–12).

185. North, *Second Isaiah*, p. 246; cf. Payne, "The Servant of the Lord," p. 142.

6

Conclusion

A SYNTHETIC PORTRAIT OF THE SERVANT

An exposition of Isaiah's Servant Songs gives four portraits of the Servant that are complementary, not contradictory. Inasmuch as Isaiah painted those portraits from a prophetic perspective that merges separate events into one picture, it is difficult to synthesize into one narrative all the data revealed about the Servant. However, at the risk of oversimplification, the following synthesis is suggested.

The Servant's story begins with His prenatal call (49:1; 42:6) and choice by Yahweh (42:1), and His identification with Yahweh as His Servant (42:1). The Servant is divinely commissioned as the true Israel to glorify Yahweh (49:3).

The Servant is prepared by Yahweh as His Disciple-Prophet (49:2; 50:4). He is committed in obedience to Yahweh (50:5) and is confident in Him (49:4). He is empowered and sustained by Yahweh through His Spirit (42:1). He is preserved, guided, and protected by Yahweh (49:2; 42:6).

The Servant is not self-promoting (42:2); He is nonviolent and gentle toward the oppressed (42:3). He is voluntarily submissive to suffering (50:6) and determined to endure suffering because of His confidence in Yahweh's aid (50:7).

The Servant is rejected by Israel (49:7; 53:1) because, seeing His unimpressive outward condition (53:2), they despise and devalue the Servant (53:3). Thus the Servant confesses His apparent initial failure but yet affirms His faith in God (49:4). Consequently, He receives a renewed call from Yahweh with an enlarged mission to deliver Gentile nations (49:6). The Servant is promised success in His mission to bring justice to the nations (42:1). That promise may have been associated with the Servant's initial call, in which case the rejection by Israel and the enlarged call to deliver Gentiles are a clarification of the historical process by which Yahweh's promise of a worldwide just order will be accomplished.

The Servant is sinlessly silent as He submits Himself to death in unjust circumstances (53:7-8), enduring inhuman disfigurement that causes Jewish consternation (52:14). In His death the Servant gives His life for sinners (53:12), bearing the corporate alienation and individual guilt of Israel (53:6), suffering as a guilt offering according to the will of Yahweh (53:6, 10), and achieving priestly purification for the Gentiles (52:15). The innocent Servant receives an honorable burial despite the intention of His enemies (53:9). The Servant who anticipated vindication by Yahweh (50:8) triumphs after death to advance the will of Yahweh (53:10).

The Servant's substitutionary redemptive sufferings are at first misunderstood by His contemporaries as sufferings which were deserved by Him (53:4, 8), but He justifies many as a result of His priestly knowledge and suffering (53:11). Having received an enlarged call to bring salvation to the Gentiles (49:5-6), the Servant becomes a light to the Gentiles (42:6). He also expects the defeat of His adversaries (50:9). The Servant regathers and establishes a new covenant with Israel (42:6; 49:9), restoring Israel spiritually to God (49:5) and physically to the land (49:8). Thus the substitutionary sufferings of the Servant are belatedly recognized as to their true character by believing Jews (53:5). The royal Servant shepherds Yahweh's needy flock (49:9-10) and causes a just order to prevail on all the earth for the nations (42:1, 3, 4). Thus the once-degraded Servant is recognized and worshiped by Gentile kings (49:7; 52:15). Thus the climax of the story sees the Servant ultimately succeeding, having endured every difficulty (42:4), having experienced Yahweh's faithfulness to bring about His ultimate success (49:7). Thus He experiences a completely fulfilled mission (49:7-12) and achieves exaltation through wise and effective action (52:13), because He had done Yahweh's will in dying as a guilt offering (53:10), and He receives victorious dominion because He died bearing the sins of many (53:12). The end of the story views the Servant's ultimate success, which brings universal praise to Yahweh (49:13), thus fulfilling His initial commission to glorify Yahweh (49:3).

THE MESSIANIC IDENTIFICATION OF THE SERVANT

The Servant of Yahweh is properly identified as Jesus the Messiah. It is not merely that some early Christians—even Jesus Himself—saw His role as like that of the Servant. Rather, as John R. Sampey has observed, "The New Testament application of this great prophecy [Isa. 52:13—53:12] to Jesus is not an accommodation of words originally spoken of Israel as a nation, but a recognition of the fact that the prophet painted in advance a portrait of which Jesus Christ is the original."[1]

Evidence for the identification of Jesus as the Servant has been presented through this study. I will now summarize that evidence.

1. *The messianic[2] interpretation of the Servant Songs clearly follows the precedent set by Jesus and the apostles.* It was concluded in chapter 1 that not only the teaching of Jesus[3] but also the

---

1. John R. Sampey, *The Heart of the Old Testament* (Nashville: Sunday School Board, SBC, 1924), pp. 172-73.
2. The term *messianic* is here used in its broad sense of reference to Jesus the Messiah, not necessarily in its more narrow sense of a royal Davidic figure.
3. Luke 22:37, citing Isaiah 53:12a; Mark 10:45, alluding to Isaiah 53:10; Mark 14:24, alluding to Isaiah 53:12; cf. more detailed treatment in chapter 1.

earliest apostolic doctrine,[4] clearly affirmed that Jesus' suffering and death were substitutionary and redemptive, in fulfillment of the Servant of Yahweh passages of Isaiah. In light of the historical events of the person and ministry of Christ and the divinely inspired record and interpretation of those events in the New Testament, it is clear that the Servant of Yahweh in Isaiah's Servant Songs is the Lord Jesus Christ.

2. *The identification of the Servant of Yahweh with Jesus the Messiah is evident in a comparison of parallels between the accomplishments of Jesus and the Servant.* As noted by F. B. Meyer (on Is. 53), "There is only one brow which this crown of thorns will fit."[5]

The following summary[6] identifies key parallels between the accomplishments of the Servant of Yahweh and the accomplishments of Jesus Christ:

(1) Both will establish a just order on all the earth (Isa. 42:1, 4; cf. Matt. 12:1-21; 25:31-46; Jude 14-15; Rev. 20:4-6).

(2) Both will mediate a new covenant for Israel, restoring Israel to God spiritually (Isa. 42:6-7; 49:5, 8-9) and to the land politically (49:8; cf. Acts 3:19-26; Rom. 11:26-27).

(3) Both will be rejected by Israel (Isa. 49:7; 53:1-3; cf. Matt. 23:37-39) and will bring the light of salvation to the Gentiles (Isa. 42:6; 49:6; cf. John 8:12; 10:16; Matt. 15:21-28;

---

4. Acts 3:13, alluding to Isaiah 52:13; Acts 3:26; 4:27, 30; 1 Peter 2:21-25 with numerous allusions to Isaiah 53 and citation of Isaiah 53:9; 2 Corinthians 5:21, alluding to Isaiah 53:6; Romans 5:19, alluding to Isaiah 53:11; Romans 4:25, alluding to Isaiah 53:12; Matthew 8:16-17, citing Isaiah 53:4; Matthew 12:18-21, citing Isaiah 42:1-4; John 1:29, alluding to Isaiah 53; John 1:23-34; John 12:38, citing Isaiah 53:1. Noteworthy also, at Christ's baptism, is God the Father's statement (Matt. 3:17), which combines Isaiah 42:1 with Psalm 2:7, thus linking the Servant figure with the Davidic king. See more detailed treatment of the above passages in chapter 1.
5. F. B. Meyer, *Christ in Isaiah: Expositions of Isaiah XL-LV* (New York: Revell, 1895), p. 158.
6. Cf. Kenneth L. Barker, "'The Servant's Story': A Study of Christ in the Four Servant Songs of Isaiah," unpublished outline, pp. 1-2; Mark A. Arrington, "The Identification of the Anonymous Servant in Isaiah 40-55" (Th.M. thesis, Dallas Theological Seminary, 1971), pp. 62-63.

28:19; Acts 28:25–28; Rom. 11:11–25; 2 Cor. 4:4–6; Eph. 3:6–8).

(4) Neither will be defeated, discouraged, or doubt Yahweh during the period of rejection by Israel (Isa. 42:4; 49:4; 50:4–9; cf. Matt. 11:25–26; John 16:33).

(5) Both will suffer vicariously for the sins of Jews and Gentiles (Isa. 52:15; 53:6; cf. 2 Cor. 5:21; Eph. 2:13–16; 1 Pet. 2:24).

(6) Both will suffer innocently (Isa. 50:8–9; 53:9; cf. John 8:46; Heb. 4:15; 7:26; 1 Pet. 2:21–23).

(7) Both will suffer silently, in submissive obedience to God's will (Isa. 53:7, 10; cf. Matt. 27:12, 14; John 4:34).

(8) Both will die as a substitutionary sacrifice and subsequently be exalted through resurrection and glorification before Yahweh (Isa. 52:13–14; 53:10–12; cf. Matt. 27:50; Luke 24:36–39; Acts 1:3; 2:33–34; Phil. 2:5–11; Heb. 1:3; 2:9; 12:2).

3. *The messianic identification of the Servant is supported by the history of the interpretation of the Servant passages.* As noted in chapter 1, the messianic view of the Servant was the unanimous Christian view until the end of the eighteenth century. Also, some form of messianic view was predominant among Jews until the twelfth-century Jewish commentators introduced the collective interpretation. The adoption of nonmessianic views among some Christian scholars grew out of the introduction of Deutero-Isaiah as the author of Isaiah 40–55 (or 66) and a general tendency among many critical scholars to reject the possibility of predictive prophecy. Those who maintain the messianic interpretation of the Servant have history on their side.

4. *The messianic interpretation of the Servant Songs is appropriate in view of the unity and theme of the book of Isaiah.* Because Isaiah is affirming the "Salvation of Yahweh through His Servant to the ends of the earth,"[7] it is to be expected that the agent of that great deliverance would be affirmed not only in the first division of the book (chaps. 1–39) but more particularly in the second division of the book (chaps. 40–66), which emphasizes

7. Alfred Martin and John A. Martin, *Isaiah: The Glory of the Messiah* (Chicago: Moody, 1983), p. 173.

the deliverance theme. Several great messianic passages do appear in the first division (see Isa. 7:1-25; 9:1-7; 11:1-16). Where in the second division of the book are the passages on the great messianic Deliverer if they are not found in the Servant Songs (and several closely related passages such as Isa. 61:1-3)?

5. *The messianic interpretation of the Servant Songs is based on a number of considerations within the Servant passages themselves,* several of which will be mentioned here.

(1) The Servant is portrayed in one passage or another (singly or jointly) in prophetic, priestly, and/or royal terminology. That corresponds to the messianic offices of Prophet, Priest and King. This argument is not forcing biblical data into the mold of systematic theology, but simply recognizes the motifs that are present in the passages. Thus the first song describes the Servant's royal characteristics; the second song, though somewhat less precise, perhaps combines royal and prophetic aspects; the third song describes His prophetic role; and the fourth song combines aspects of His prophetic and priestly work. Thus the combined portrait of the Servant includes characteristics of the threefold office of Christ.

(2) Numerous characteristics or actions of the Servant are ascribed in other prophetic passages to the Messiah. Like the Servant, the Messiah is committed to and discipled by Yahweh (Isa. 11:2; Ps. 40:6-8); is described in horticultural terms (Isa. 11:1; Zech. 3:8); accomplishes His work through the empowerment of Yahweh's Spirit (Isa. 11:2; cf. 61:1-3); is meek and humble (Zech. 9:9) and deals gently with the oppressed (Isa. 11:3-5; 61:1-2; Ps. 72:2-4, 12-14); restores Israel to God and to the land (Isa. 11:12; Hos. 1:10-11; 3:5; Amos 9:11-15; cf. Dan. 7:13-14); leads Israel like a shepherd (Ezek. 34:23-24; 37:20-25; Micah 5:4; cf. Zech. 13:7); delivers spiritually blind prisoners (Isa. 9:2-6); brings the light of salvation to the Gentiles (Ps. 72:17; Isa. 11:1-2); causes a just and righteous order to prevail among the nations (Isa. 9:7; 11:3-5, 10; Ps. 2:8-9; 45:6; Zech. 9:10); endures suffering and death (Ps. 22:12-28; Zech. 13:7); is not abandoned to the grave (Ps. 16:10); is vindicated by Yahweh (Ps. 22:24); and partakes of the spoils of victory (Ps. 68:18).

(3) The attributes of the Servant's ministry preclude accomplishment by any lesser figure than the Messiah. This is true with regard to its universal scope (Isa. 42:1, 4; 49:6-7, 12; 52:15); the certainty of its ultimate accomplishment (cf. the divine pronouncements in 42:1-4); its redemptive purpose and spiritual consequences (cf. 42:4b, 6b-7; 49:6b, 8; 50:10-11; 52:15; 53:4-6, 8, 10-12); its culmination in His sacrificial and substitutionary death (53:4-6, 8-12); and its relation to the fulfillment of Israel's covenants: the land promises (49:8), the national promises (49:6, 8-12), the throne promises (implied in the task of establishing justice, 42:1, 3, 4), and the redemptive promises of the New Covenant for Israel (cf. 42:6; 49:8).

It is concluded that the Servant of Isaiah's Songs is indeed the Lord Jesus Christ. This identification is supported by the New Testament precedent, the parallels with Jesus' ministry, the history of interpretation, the unity and theme of the book of Isaiah, and a number of considerations found in the Servant Songs, including their portrait of the threefold office of Messiah, their harmony with other messianic passages, and their description of the Servant's far-reaching accomplishments.

Selected Bibliography

Alexander, Joseph Addison. *Commentary on the Prophecies of Isaiah*. Grand Rapids: Zondervan, 1953.

Birks, T. R. *Commentary on the Book of Isaiah*. London: Rivingtons, 1871.

Blocher, Henri. *Songs of the Servant*. Downers Grove, Ill.: InterVarsity, 1975.

Culver, Robert D. *The Sufferings and the Glory of the Lord's Righteous Servant*. Minneapolis: Christian Service Foundation, 1958.

Delitzsch, Franz J. *Isaiah*. Commentary on the Old Testament. Grand Rapids: Eerdmans, 1973.

France, R. T. *Jesus and the Old Testament: His Application of Old Testament Passages to Himself and His Mission*. Grand Rapids: Baker, 1982.

Hengstenberg, E. W. *Christology of the Old Testament and a Commentary on the Messianic Predictions*. Grand Rapids: Kregel, 1956.

Kay, W. "Isaiah: Introduction, Commentary and Critical Notes," in *The Bible Commentary*. Edited by F. C. Cook. Vol. 5. Grand Rapids: Baker, 1981.

Kelley, Page H. "Isaiah," in *The Broadman Bible Commentary.* Edited by C. J. Allen. Vol. 5. Nashville: Broadman, 1971.

Knight, George A. F. *Deutero-Isaiah: A Theological Commentary on Isaiah 40—55.* Nashville: Abingdon, 1965.

Leupold, H. C. *Exposition of Isaiah.* Grand Rapids: Baker, 1971.

MacRae, Allan A. *The Gospel of Isaiah.* Chicago: Moody, 1977.

Martin, Alfred, and Martin, John A. *Isaiah: The Glory of the Messiah.* Chicago: Moody, 1983.

McKenzie, John L. *Second Isaiah.* The Anchor Bible. New York: Doubleday, 1968.

Melugin, Roy F. *The Formation of Isaiah 40—55.* New York: Walter de Gruyter, 1976.

Muilenburg, James. "The Book of Isaiah: Chapters 40—66," in *The Interpreter's Bible.* Edited by George A. Buttrick. Vol. 5. Nashville: Abingdon, 1956.

North, Christopher R. *The Second Isaiah: Introduction, Translation, and Commentary to Chapters XL—LV.* Clarendon, Tex.: Clarendon, 1964.

North, Christopher R. *The Suffering Servant in Deutero-Isaiah: An Historical and Critical Study.* 2d ed. London: Oxford U., 1956.

Odendaal, Dirk H. *The Eschatological Expectation of Isaiah 40—66 with Special Reference to Israel and the Nations.* Phillipsburg, N.J.: Presbyterian and Reformed, 1970.

Payne, David F. "Isaiah," in *The New Layman's Bible Commentary.* Edited by G. C. D. Howley, F. F. Bruce, and H. L. Ellisen. Grand Rapids: Zondervan, 1979.

Pieper, August. *Isaiah II: An Exposition of Isaiah 40—66.* Milwaukee: Northwestern, 1979.

Rowley, H. H. *The Servant of the Lord and Other Essays on the Old Testament,* 2d ed. Oxford: Basil Blackwell, 1952.

Unger, Merrill F. *Unger's Commentary on the Old Testament,* 2 vols. Chicago: Moody, 1982.

Urwick, William. *The Servant of Jehovah: A Commentary, Grammatical and Critical, Upon Isaiah LII. 13—LIII. 12.* Edinburgh: T. & T. Clark, 1877.

Westermann, Claus. *Isaiah 40—66: A Commentary.* Philadelphia: Westminster, 1975.

Whybray, R. N. *Isaiah 40—66*. New Century Bible Commentary. Grand Rapids: Eerdmans, 1981.

Whybray, R. N. *Thanksgiving for a Liberated Prophet: An Interpretation of Isaiah Chapter 53*. Sheffield: Journal for the Study of Old Testament, 1978.

Young, Edward J. *The Book of Isaiah: The English Text, with Introduction, Exposition, and Notes*, 3 vols. Grand Rapids: Eerdmans, 1965-72.

Subject Index

Abraham, 2, 7
Abrahamic covenant, 2, 19, 27
Ahaz, 17
Ancestor ideology, 15
Apostles' teaching, 6–8
Assyria, 17, 19, 25, 26
Assyrian captivity, 25, 27, 74
Atonement, 108

Babylon, 17, 19, 25, 26, 57, 69, 74, 111
Babylonian captivity/Exile, 17–19, 25, 27, 35, 52, 54, 55, 75, 123
Bethlehem, 31
Branch, 30, 31

Christ. See Messiah; Jesus Christ
Christology, 8
Comfort (divine), 19, 60, 77
Corporate personality, 11, 14, 15
Covenants, 5, 19. See also
    Abrahamic covenant;

Davidic covenant; New
    covenant; Sinaitic covenant
Covenant lawsuit, 21
Cyrus, 9, 14, 20, 26, 36, 52, 56, 57, 74

David, 2, 3, 33, 35, 39
Davidic covenant, 19, 27, 29, 30, 33, 55
Davidic line/dynasty, 2, 10, 28, 32, 42
Day of the Lord, 28
Deliverance, 35
Deutero-Isaiah, 3, 9, 13, 14, 16–18, 36, 99, 111
Disputation, 35

Egypt, 25, 57
Eleazer, 9, 14
Enthronement psalms, 33, 34
Eschatology of Isaiah, 23–28
Eternal state, 27, 29
Exile. See Babylonian captivity

Author Index

Scripture Index

Index of Hebrew and Greek Words

HEBREW WORDS

'āshām, 5
bᵉrît, 53
bᵉṣedek, 52
gō'ēl, 26, 72
gôy(îm), 53, 73
dābār, 127
dākā', 121
dôr, 127
hā'ēl yhwh, 51
hinnēh, 101
wᵉhû', 125
ḥālāl, 121
yhwh, 1, 2, 21, 51
yhwh ṣᵉbā'ôt, 21
yazzeh, 105, 107
yaṣdîq, 136
yāśîm, 49
yaśkîl, 102, 103
yôṣi', 44
yiqpᵉṣû, 105

ka'ᵃsher, 104
kēn, 104
kullānû, 123
le'ᵉmet, 48
limmûdîm, 83
lô, 69
lō, 69
māshaḥtî, 107
mᵉlākîm, 105
mî, 92
min, 107
mishḥāt, 107
mishpāt, 40, 43–45, 49, 67, 68
nāgaʿ, 120
nāgaś, 125
nāzâ, 107
naᶜᵃneh, 125
napsho, 132
nāśā', 46
nāthattî, 42
nēgaᶜ, 120
nepesh, 73

GREEK WORDS